ESCAPE FROM VIETNAM

ESCAPE
FROM
VIETNAM

THE STORY OF DOAN

By DOAN

TRANSLATED BY CARMEN LANDRY

OPTIMUM PUBLISHING INTERNATIONAL INC
MONTREAL . TORONTO

Published by Optimum Publishing International (1984) Inc. Montreal

Legal deposit 2nd quarter 1988
National Library of Canada
Legal deposit 2nd trimester 1988
Bibliothèque nationale du Québec

Canadian Cataloguing in Publication Data

Doan, 1964 –
Escape From Vietnam

Translation of: L'eau de la liberté.

ISBN 0-88890-186-0

1. Doan, 1964 – 2. Refugees, Political – Vietnam –
biography. 3. Refugees, Political – Quebec (Province) –
Biography. I. Title.
DS559.5.D6213 1987 325'.21'0924 C87-090059-5

Translated by Carmen Landry
Cover Design by Pierre Legault
Edited by Laurel Sullivan.

Printed and bound in Canada

For information, address:
Optimum Publishing International (1984) Inc.
4255 Ste-Catherine W., Suite 100
Montréal, Québec
H3Z 1P7
Michael S. Baxendale, President

To my two families, the one in Vietnam who gave me the chance to be free and the one in Canada who gave me their love, and to my brother, Thanh, who shared this journey with me.

CHAPTER 1

SUNDAY, APRIL 27, 1975

WAR

As sounds of distant cannons and artillery fire echo in our ears, we help Mother prepare the evening meal. Her distressing silence is so uncommon that it burdens the atmosphere. She peers over at us, then quickly lowers her head. As the howling voices of the cannons grow louder and louder, we plunge deeper into silence.

Sitting at the dinner table, with Father present, the situation seems even more ominous. After saying grace, he whispers something to my mother. I overhear that the Vietcong are not far away and that the war is raging almost everywhere. Again, a veil of silence enshrouds us and I wonder who these Vietcong could be.

I am suffocating in this atmosphere. Only my three-month old brother seems to be enjoying the tingling sensation of the thunderous shelling, gurgling with glee as he plays with his toy. My two-year old sister is pouting because father is not giving her his usual attention. We, the older ones, share our parents' anguish for they know the fear of war. It also scares the children because it represents the unknown.

Saigon had been far removed from the battle now raging at our doorstep.

I know that for many people, war brings to mind some horrible memories. I have cried for the baby that suckled its mother's corpse lying by the roadside, as the weapons of war continued to fire.

I have seen my cousin's body brought back from the war zone, grimacing, in a coffin draped with a flag the color of his blood.

My girlfriend used to tell me about her father's adventures flying a plane above the clouds and mountain ranges. Sometimes, he would bring her back a plant for her collection or a rare flower. But one day, my friend came to school wearing a white blouse decorated with a small black square, a symbol of mourning. I knew then, she would never again speak of her collection or her father's adventures.

We had always longed to meet our paternal grandparents who lived in North Vietnam. Mother had promised that we would visit them as soon as peace returned to our land. "When will peace come?" we would ask and she would reply: "When men tire of making war, they will make peace." Impatiently, we awaited that day, confident that it would soon come. But one day, a letter arrived and the news it brought put an end to our long-awaited dream: our grandparents were dead!

I have shed many tears for my grandparents and for my shattered dreams of peace. But tonight, the fear and dread of war is, more than ever, a reality that I must face.

There is none of the usual mealtime bantering tonight. Everyone is lost in their own thoughts. With one ear pressed to the radio speaker, Father listens to the news. By the change of expression on his face, Mother can guess what is happening. Once the news is over, he turns off the radio and gives my mother a brief account of what he heard. It seems that there is fighting going on in almost every suburb of Saigon. As Father speaks, the roaring cannons and fusilade blasts punctuate his words. I glance out the window: the street is deserted and threatens with death anyone who would dare to venture outside. All doors are firmly shut. Without hesitation, I lock up ours too.

Tonight, all seven of us sleep huddled between our parents, underneath the two beds on which we have piled blankets, cushions and clothing to protect us against the bombs. We say our evening prayers and Mother asks us to offer up our lives to the Lord, for this night does not belong to us...After prayers, Father recommends that we sleep, for who knows what tomorrow may bring. Perhaps better or worse things...nobody knows. Suddenly, we are all paralyzed into silence as the bombardments begin again – louder and closer. Grasping my sister's hand, I whisper in her ear to ask if she is afraid. No answer. She is already asleep! Drowsiness finally overcomes me.

This morning, we wake up around six o'clock. I look around to make sure we are all alive and well. My next thought is: what if I had died in the night? Then I realize that the bombings have stopped. While helping Mother prepare breakfast, Father walks in looking distraught. He said that last night, near our home, a family of eight had been killed by a bomb. A painful sensation shakes me. I grab my baby brother in my arms and hold him tightly as though someone were trying to take him away from me.

During the day, truckloads of soldiers and tanks parade down the street as if it were National Day but they seem to be in a hurry. Helicopters are hovering in the sky, watching our every move. Here and there, groups of men gather outside their doors, discussing what they call "politics". As they carry on with their daily chores, the women discreetly exchange the bits of news that have been circulating from every corner of town. The children have no school today, but nobody has the heart to go out to play. We all remain indoors, eyes glued to the screened door in order not to miss anything. Only the cries of the peddlers provide us with a sense of normalcy but, if we listen closely, something is still amiss. The shops are open, but the owners are more involved in talking than in selling their wares.

Our house is located near the Tan Son Nhat airport, the country's major military airport. It is the main focus of all the attacks and its destiny will determine that of the government. We are prisoners condemned to die. The outer shell of our little house is made of concrete, its wooden skeleton is topped with tin. It could never resist a bombing. Three of its sides are so well flanked by other houses that, should a fire start at the other end of our district, our home would surely burn down in a matter of minutes. Where can we possibly go to avoid danger?

Twenty days ago, when the war had begun to rage on the outskirts of Saigon, we tried to escape by heading towards the sea. In a bus, packed like sardines, we ventured out on a road where landmines had been hidden to surprise us. The driver could do nothing but forge ahead on this perilous route. I was sick. I vomited so much that I feared turning inside out of my skin. Finally, we reached the seashore, the frontier between peace and war. We waited, hoped, and reached out for a place of refuge beyond the sea where there would be everlasting peace.

To ward off the mass exodus, our country's leaders promised that victory was at hand. They also reiterated their profound attachment to the people and to the nation, vowing to valiantly risk their lives to defend them. This assurance put an end to our escape plans, because for a Vietnamese, leaving his country means giving up a part of his soul. I did not care to undertake such a voyage. Hoping for victory, my parents decided to take us all back home. But that very night, a new president was named. Those who had spoken of victory, solidarity and fraternity had already used their tickets to freedom.

In no time at all, three successive presidents were in power. And we, as helpless as fish on a cutting board, what could we do? Absolutely nothing! That is why on this 28th day of April, we stopped running away from the threatening ravages of war.

Because our house is not safe enough, my father swallows his pride and humbly begs a wealthy lady, who owns a three-story building in our area, to grant us shelter. This woman is a renowned green-eyed monster adept at flattery and scorn. Normally she would not even look at my father but today, since it is a matter of life and death, she takes us in.

That night about a dozen families take refuge in a room on the main floor of "moneybags" house. The children moan while the grown-ups quietly mumble to themselves nervously fingering their rosary beads. As the bombs blast their fury, deafening noises accompany the phantasmagoric lights created by the explosions. Every minute in this place seems like a century to me. I am tired of listening to these people pray – they who were always critical of my family. But strangely enough, I am praying too.

The sounds of war jolt me back to reality. Death lurks nearby. Her impending presence quickly dissipates all my prejudiced opinions about these malevolent neighbors. Suddenly, I feel very relieved that I can find it in my heart to forgive them. I am even amazed at my generosity. But does a person have to be in this type of situation to drop her mask of pride and grant a simple pardon? I am guilt-ridden by this thought.

While we are barricaded in this house, we cannot tell night from day. When the bombings momentarily stop, my parents dash over to our house to get some food. In their absence, I am in charge of my brothers and sisters, since I am the eldest. We are seven children. Myself (I am eleven), my brother Thanh who's ten years old, my four sisters: Ly, Kim, Mai, Thu and my baby brother Tin who is only a few months old. Seldom do we ever sit around so quietly with nothing to do all day.

In better times, our favourite family activity is putting on plays. We love to act out the various roles of doctor-patient, mother-father, teacher-students, cops-'n-robbers, ghosts and travellers. The bed becomes our stage and we use blankets as curtains, flowers and old clothes as costumes. Our only spectators are Mother and Father – our best public. The most popular play of all is one which we produce every year and where I play the role of Mary; Thanh becomes Joseph; Ly is Santa Claus; my baby brother or sister play Jesus; and the others are Three Kings of Orient. Over the years, I have discovered during these playful times that Ly is gifted in directing, Thanh in decoration, Mai in singing and Thu in comedy. Together, we make great team!

But today, bunched up in a corner of the room, we await the conclusion of this real life play performed and produced by grown-up actors. Thanh, our doctor-father-robber-ghost, cannot portray these figures of war. Neither can the other children. We look more like sad and helpless puppies, just like our dog, Kéo, who is all alone at home. Every minute or so, my sisters ask where Mother is and they cry. The baby is very unhappy because he is hungry and Mother is not here...I am tired of having to comfort them all.

My parents arrive to give us something to eat, relating details of what they saw and heard. Thanh and I would love to go out and see for ourselves, but they say it is still too dangerous. They seem confident that the fighting will soon be over. Most of the country's leaders have fled. Only a few groups of volunteer fighters are left to defend the city and the North Vietnamese army is beginning to march into Saigon.

I am glad the war is over, no matter who won it; as long as there is peace. But my parents look more worried than relieved. They speak to each other in hushed tones. I think I know why. They, themselves, were refugees from North Vietnam after the Geneva Convention was signed in 1954. Leaving everything behind, they risked their lives to come and settle in the South. They wanted to be free! Free to work; to find happiness; and to make a better future for themselves. For my parents, today's victory by the North means reliving the same nightmare all over again. Don't the North Vietnamese realize that the exodus of thousands indicates to the whole world that the new system is doomed to failure? No wonder my parents are so worried: for a second time, the lasso is being swung around an already wounded beast...

We are still waiting... Our parents come and go. Around one o'clock in the afternoon, the atmosphere and the oppressive heat in this room become unbearable. Suddenly, a man appears at the door with a beaming smile on his face. At the top of his voice, he informs us that the revolution has reached its objective: the South has been liberated, a provisional government is in place and the unification of the country is imminent. I know this man and I am stunned by what he is saying. He is a South Vietnamese, which explains his enthusiasm: he has never lived under a communist regime like my parents have.

I remain quite indifferent to the excited crowd rushing out the door. Can a thirty-year war cleanse a nation of greed, inflation, segregation, social-class conflicts, prostitution and drugs? I wonder! My father starts picking up our belongings; Mother takes the baby in her arms; we children remain dazed and immobile. Mother gently reassures us by saying: "It's all over now, we can go home." Although she is smiling, her eyes look troubled and sad. I know she is not convinced that our troubles are over. They are just beginning. I get up, dragging my two sisters along by the hand, with a firm resolve in my heart that no one, but no one, would ever hurt my family. I would destroy them all if they tried. I remember a story about a hero who risked his life to save his castle. I would be just as brave!

CHAPTER 2

HOME

The streets of Saigon look quite different today than they did two days ago. Amid the chaos, hundreds of flags wave from windows and doorways flaunting their bright yellow stars. People are walking down the street, greeting one another with a smile, happy to see each other again after so long. Others exchange material with which to make new flags. Cars bearing banners, flowers, ribbons and flags go streaming down the road. I see many familiar faces. Most of them have never seen the spectre of communism.

All this fanfare reminds me of a spring fair. Mother, too, is in a festive mood although her patriotic fervour is clouded by darker memories of North Vietnam. She says she will make a flag of her own when we are home but there is no enthusiasm in her voice. Mother hurries back to our house while my sisters and I dawdle along trying to absorb all the changes in our neighbourhood. I see my first soldier from the North. He is dressed in camouflage fatigues with a gun at his side but he is wearing ordinary rubber sandals. A few peasants stop to talk to him. Perhaps they are discussing the latest offensive or wondering where he is from. Since we are walking right past him, I can observe him more closely. He is young – very young – and, standing there awkwardly rigid with gun in hand, he looks like a calf whose horns have barely begun to sprout. Smiling timidly, he answers the people's questions. I am struck by his accent. When he says he hasn't seen his family in five years, I feel sorry for him because I was away from my family once, for three days, and I was unconsolable the whole time. Imagine – five years!

After the others move on, we are left alone to face the soldier. Trembling with fear, I quickly prop up my brother who is starting to feel heavy in my arms and I urge my sisters to move along home. A sense of foreboding washes over me.

When we arrive, Mother is sitting at the sewing machine finishing her flag and Father is busy working near our aquarium. As we approach him, he demands to know what took us so long to get home. I tell him we stopped to listen to what the soldier had to say. No scolding follows, but he says he got home just in time to save one of the fishes that had jumped out of the water. He temporarily places the fish in a large pail while he cleans out the aquarium and we slowly count each one. We really love our aquatic pets. We used to have hundreds of them, in all shapes and colors. Often, when we came home from school, Father would have a surprise for us: a new and brightly-coloured friend would be dancing and wiggling its fine tail at us through the window of its glass house. During our absence, half of them have died and only twenty are left. The Zebra, our biggest one, is barely breathing at the bottom of the bowl. He is a widower now. I feel very sad and angry because these little creatures never hurt anyone. So why should they be victims of war? Outside, someone is shouting "Liberation", but from what will I be liberated? Father has been silent for some time now and when I ask him if he plans to buy more fishes, he simply answers "yes". But I am not sure he was really answering my question.

We children continue with our inspection of the whole house and proceed to put things back in place. We moved to our house almost a year ago and she became very dear to all of us. Our house was a storeroom of fairy tales, stories and songs. She was like a brand new hope chest in which all our memories, habits and emotions were securely in place and, over the past few days, the contents of our chest have been tossed about. We must now tidy up and securely put our dreams and feelings back in place. Beneath my feet, the coolness of the tiles reminds me of the simple and quiet life we once had.

Our poor house looks lonely after being totally abandoned for two days. She is sulking...but I assure her that from now on, we will always be with her. I will never never leave you again, my friend, my home!.

My mother explains to me that social, political and cultural structures are rebuilt after a coup d'état. Society is in a turmoil and public administrators are in limbo for days following the shift in power.

Since there is no school today, I go out and join the other children in the neighbourhood to talk about what happened. I notice that some of them are missing. Someone says they have fled across the border. We think they are the lucky ones, but why? The smartest in the group says that children in the United States don't work like we do. They don't even dress, eat, play or go to school the same way we do. How do they live, these children from other countries? Nobody seems to know for sure. In any case, I am not sure I would want to live in a country where nothing is the same as it is here.

CHAPTER 3

POST-WAR SAIGON

The young people in my neighbourhood spend a lot of time together discussing and arguing. Some say that many soldiers who were loyal to the former army are hiding here and there, and that weapons are buried almost everywhere. From one day to the next, our topics of conversation become increasingly terrifying and horrible. And when we have nothing more to talk about, everybody goes home.

I have to watch the children so that Mother can prepare dinner. While she is busy cooking, she informs us that Grandmother and my uncles' families are all well. Both my uncles – one was a military teacher and the other, a traffic officer – were called back to their stations and forced to hand in their weapons. Not long ago, when South Vietnamese troops were being marched down the streets at gunpoint, we had a chance to see and talk to them along the route. They are my mother's brothers. The eldest, the policeman, is a short, scrawny and straight-faced person; whereas the younger one is tall, hairy and very funny...even when he is sad, as he was then. But neither one would ever hurt anybody.

When my 'funny' uncle saw the tears and worried look on my mother's face, he smiled and said consolingly, "My dear big sister, you know I never wanted to be a soldier. So don't cry, because tomorrow, I will be relieved of that duty." Meanwhile, my 'straight-faced' uncle looked as glum as a rainy day in autumn...he didn't say a word. A week later, all these soldiers were marched deep into the woods where they were to be subjected to a "re-education program in political science". They were sent off without any baggage and without the chance to say good-bye to their families. I hear it whispered that every day in these supervised camps, the prisoners undergo some kind of brainwashing, do hard labour and try to cope with life in the wilderness. Since my uncle, the policeman, was not a well-educated man, and had never used firearms, he was not subjected to this torture.

Peace! Does it exist somewhere? And for whom? There is no point venting my anger and disgust since it can't relieve anyone else's suffering. Even this afternoon, the children rushed over to watch a thief being executed. I just can't believe all this is happening. Such public executions often occur now. Even though they are thieves, I feel sorry for these people. Hasn't the war caused enough killing and suffering? It doesn't make sense to shoot every single criminal! The Dai-Loi Hotel – a former American base – was transformed into a prison. The desperate cries, howls, shrieks, and gunshots which pierce its walls at night, terrify me. Sometimes I wonder where they find all the people to fill that six-story building. We never hear talk of trials or courts of justice; it is true that our university has no Faculty of Law.

Everything is changed! For better or for worse? Everywhere, from North to South, a new government and a new regime has been set up. Bit by bit, social order is slowly returning. We must go back to school to finish the year which the war so brutally interrupted. We salute a new flag; sing a new national anthem; and speak a new language. We don't even live in Saigon anymore, but in Hô Chi Minh City. All these changes make me realize that my dream of becoming as strong and as brave as a soldier is nothing but an illusion. This noble ideal of wanting to risk my life for my country lies buried beneath the ruins of homes, villages and cities devasted by bombs. I was never ashamed to sing the old national anthem, but today, singing our new anthem, I feel I am dishonoring all those whose blood was spilled during this war. It also makes me very uneasy to have to use the term "Uncle" when speaking of our past or current president. Every acceptable speech must now begin with "Thanks to Uncle Hô and the Party..."

My father has gone back to work. He is a school teacher who used to teach in several private Catholic schools in Saigon but, at present, under the socialist regime, all schools are public and non-denominational. So he only teaches in one school and he must hide the fact that he used to write articles for a Catholic newspaper. It could get him into trouble.

Under the new regime, educated people are labelled – undesirable – because they are "reactionaries with corrupt ideas". Even the teachers are obliged to take courses in political science. This brainwashing has no effect on experienced scholars like my father. I don't know why, but he is often in a bad mood when he comes home from school. In addition to his job, he has been named District Representative, which keeps him away from us at night, too.

In order to maintain peace in this nation, and to have better control over the people, the government has divided the country into districts. Everyone is under surveillance, even the children and the elderly. Each category of people must attend a weekly meeting where attendance is strictly taken. Because of this, our family is divided and we no longer have any time to enjoy life together. Our fairy tales and songs have died with the new regime. Poverty overshadows our sunny childhood days and all our energy is focused on our daily ration of rice.

My mother has started to sell off everything she can. In tears, we beg her not to sell our small TV set which replaces the wonderful tales and adventures our parents used to have to time to tell us. But she needs a great deal of money. Almost everything has to be bought on the black market and it is very expensive. Anyway, everybody is getting rid of their electrical applicances or other luxury items so that nobody can suspect them of being capitalists. According to the government, people in the South have been living in too much luxury. But strangely enough, it is people from the North who are buying up what we sell – they who vowed to free us from the dreadful misery brought on by the American imperialists!

My father's teaching salary is not sufficient to feed the family. His wages have been determined by the government and they don't even cover the cost of rice and meat. Now that I am twelve, I can work like an adult. Having to watch my parents struggle so hard without doing my share to help put food on our table has become unbearable. I know how I can make money! I grab the water kettle and ask my mother for 50 cents, promising to bring home more money by the end of the day. After preparing some iced tea, my sister and I eagerly set out, whistling, with kettle in hand, one glass, a pail of water to rinse it out, and the tea. As I enter the adult world, I feel so proud to be useful at last. We are both extremely happy because now we will be rich!

"Iced Tea! Iced tea!" we shout at the top of our voices as we walk through the marketplace. Many other children are doing the same thing, so we must yell louder and run faster to catch up with our thirsty customers. By the end of the afternoon, we have hardly any voice left, our legs are tired and wobbly, and all we have in our pockets is 70 cents. The merchants are closing up shop, so we head back home. Just by the look on our faces, Mother quickly surmises what profits our first day in business produced.

No, it is not easy to earn a living. But still, I manage to convince my mother to let us try something else. Using my brother's baby carriage, we become real street vendors, selling wood, bananas, cookies and other sundries that are sold on every street corner. But since we so desperately need the very things we are trying to sell, I soon realize that this is not such a good idea.

Always I wait for that promised peace to come...but around me, I find nothing but sorrow and misery. This afternoon, I went with several classmates to burn some incense on our teacher's grave. Why did she have to leave us so soon? In accordance with government policy, our professor had no choice but to go to her local health clinic to have her baby. Because this center was ill-equipped, both technically and professionally, they could only save the baby. She shouldn't have died! I know her husband. He is my brother's teacher. Alas, water flows to the river, money goes to the rich and tragedy strikes the poor...

After a long discussion with my mother, Father decides to open a bicycle parts shop in the front of our house. Since he is still teaching, I am in charge of the shop after classes. This is all new to me but in time I get to know the name, function, and price of each intricate part of a bicycle. I know exactly what to say in order to get my price and how to write up bills. In the evening, I balance the books and determine what supplies we need and where to buy them. But before long, almost two out of every three houses on our street are selling these same things. This time, I am really discouraged because the failure is double--my shop and my studies. How can I possibly study when I have to be in school all morning, work at the shop in the afternoon, and balance the books at night? Through sheer luck, I managed to complete grade six, but things don't look very promising for the seventh grade.

While I try to catch up on my studies, Mother now handles the few clients we have. She also does dental work of sorts, using oriental techniques, and offers skin-care treatments, but her clients are rare. I simply can't understand why nothing is working out; plants are closing down everywhere and so are many businesses.

Yet our troubles are just beginning. In our area, thieves and prostitutes reign like kings and queens. Every night, someone gets robbed. Keo's bark often wakes me, and I can hear the pilferers crawling over the rooftops. It is terrifying because I am told that they have knives and that they are the ones who smash the street lights to avoid being seen practicing their trade.

When the city lights dim, the world of prostitution comes alive. In front of our door at night, it is like a masquerade ball. Hundreds of women are assembled while the men stroll among them, eyeing each one as though they were attending a slave auction. When the police arrive, everyone disappears, but ten minutes later, they are all back on the streets again.

My mother doesn't want us to watch such a spectacle. I know that what they do in the darkness is not very nice, but what exactly do they do? Mother says I don't need to know. These parties last until midnight or one o'clock in the morning. Their rowdy laughter and ribaldry disturbs our sleep. Mother says that prostitution has always existed, surreptitiously like the devil, but when times are hard, like now, this evil is more prevalent. Behind prostitution and thievery lies a rampant drug problem – three insidious diseases gnawing away at our society.

CHAPTER 4

MY FATHER

When the government officials make their rounds of inspection in our district, my father, being the representative for the citizens living in our area, must report to them. No matter what he does, he is in a bind: if he denounces anyone in one of his reports, that person will threaten him; if he refuses to do so, he will be accused of being unfaithful to the Party. Before he had the chance to find a solution to this dilemma, a woman owning a lumber business came over to the house while he was at school, and insulted my mother. "If your husband's job as a merchant of words is not enough for you to live on, I'll give you food, but he must stop spying on us like an owl...Either he leaves my business alone, or else you'll never have peace with me." she said. We didn't understand any of this.

After tonight's meeting of the District Representatives' Commission, Father was unusually quiet. We later learn that he has handed in his resignation to the Commission, out of honesty and self-respect. He had accepted this responsibility without pay; now he is risking his life to redeem his past as an ordinary professor who has always defended the truth and he is afraid.

One day, while I was fooling around with my brother, I called him "My Comrade" (an expression used by the Vietcong), and my father scowled at me. Father's looks scare me now. In the past, whenever I did something wrong, he would always chastise me with kind words and his punishments were reasonable, never cruel. Now anguish and fear seem to have taken hold of my father's body and soul.

Father became depressed and sick last month. His illness is rather strange; he doesn't eat, doesn't sleep, doesn't talk. All he does is write, in the dark, about being persecuted, reprimanded and suspected of being a spy. I don't understand all this, but maybe it is true. He often sends us to the neighbours to apologize for him. Now he is completely exhausted and his body is bloated. He just lies there, straight as a board, eyes shut, not saying a word when we gather round his bed to pray. Nothing can stem the flow of our tears because we are afraid he will leave us for good. From day to day his condition grows worse.

Sometimes my mother runs out at night to borrow money so she can buy him the necessary medicine on the black market, while I go knocking on the doctor's door. He doesn't like to be disturbed so late at night, so I have to cry and beg him to come. I am terrified of the dark, but my father is more important to me than anything else in the world.

We cry often and we pray. His physical state is showing a marked improvement, but his psychological state is worsening. He becomes violent and aggressive; he beats up my mother and says the most terrible and unimaginable things to her. He even accuses her of being unfaithful to him, of wanting to kill him so that she can marry the neighbour. He lost his teaching job and keeps asking Mother for money to buy food for himself. But before she can give him any, she has to try and sell something in the house. Often, when she sends me to the market, I come back with only the money because meat and vegetables cost more than what she has given me to spend.

Father doesn't understand why she can't comply with his requests for money and food. Every time she refuses, he beats her or threatens her with a knife. We come to her rescue, begging him to stop, but his anger drowns out our cries. I have hidden everything in the house that resembles a knife. In a tearful voice, mother pleads with us on his behalf, "Children, you know your father has never raised a hand to me before. But today, because times are so hard, he is very sick. I will always love him. God has united us and I know He will help me bear this cross."

I can understand my mother, but Father's condition gets worse every day. He still believes he is being persecuted and grows wary of everybody. He has become so strange and mysterious, I am afraid of him. Fearing that someone is trying to poison him, he prepares his own food in the bathroom. To give my mother a good scare, he hid my young brother and sister. Afterwards, the children told us that he bought them some candy and let them play in the nearby cemetery. Now we have to follow him, at a distance, when he leaves the house with the children.

It is as though someone else has taken possession of his body. Occasionally, he gets down on his knees in front of people and begs them not to kill him. He also annoys the women in the street and gets very angry with the customers. We are always having to make excuses for the trouble he causes. Some neighbours say he is only "playing the fool" so he can talk all the nonsense he wants. This sparks more arguments and fights. Often, people gang together to beat him and nobody tries to intervene. My brother, my sister and I are the only ones who ever come to his defense; we jump on the men, scratching, kicking and punching them as hard as we can, while my younger sisters run home crying and shouting for help.

In such instances, I feel so brave and strong that I am not afraid of anything, not even a man who is much bigger and stronger than me. We attack with such force, that the enemy finally retreats. Mother comes to help him get up and takes him home. We follow, leaving behind us the disparaging remarks of those vicious tongues.

They don't like my father because he knows too much; they even rejoice in the fact that he is sick. It hurts me when they call him the "big marble statue" or the "fool". Even the children learn these words from their parents and use them to scorn my father. It is true that he is sick and fat, but he is my father, our father, and we love him. Nobody has the right to treat him like that!

Most of the time when people hurl rocks at us, spit on us, or call us names, we simply walk on with our heads down, feigning indifference. Mother says that Jesus himself, the Son of God, accepted such scorn so that we might be saved. But I am not Jesus and whenever I have the chance to get my revenge, I take it.

Since Father can't work and Mother has no real trade, each one of us tries to earn some money. In the morning, out on the streets, I sell eggs and vegetables, but the police never leave me alone. They want me to pay taxes, so I run away when they show up. Often, when I can't sell all my produce, Mother gets upset and suggests that I leave school and go to work. I am really heartbroken, but I know she is tired of having to feed a family of seven and take care of a sick husband. Sometimes our only meal of the day consists of a bit of boiled manioca with a pinch of salt. Having to cope with so many problems, leads her to the brink of despair. Sometimes she says to us, "If it weren't for you, my precious children, I would have jumped off the Binh Triêu bridge long ago".

CHAPTER 5

REVOLT

Although I sell eggs, very seldom do we get to eat some ourselves. To satisfy our appetites, we add all sorts of things to the rice in order to stretch it a little. One grows accustomed to everything! At mealtime, I am never really hungry because I am too tired. Why hang on to life when life merely consists of earning your daily bread? I think it is absurd to live like this, but we still hang on...and we hope. For me, however, going hungry is not as bad as being poorly dressed. Mother can't afford to buy clothes and we only have one outfit each, we have to wash it out every evening. So much the better if a gentle breeze dries our clothes during the night, and too bad if they are still damp in the morning: we have to wear them anyway.

I have no idea where life is leading us. The rebukes, the scorn, and misery to which we are exposed fill me with revolt. It is not a crime to be poor! The school yard is the only place where I can vent my anger against those who rile me, for here, outside my district, my parents are not implicated.

The seething hatred in my heart often explodes. Violence is my only mode of expression. When the boys taunt me at school, I respond with my fists. And when I fight with these boys, I know just how to hurt them.

Sometimes they call me a thief. Since I am always angry and sullen, the girls call me the "grumpy shtroumpf". But the violence doesn't solve anything! All I want is to be admired by my friends, not to be treated like trash. I am a somebody and I know it. That is why I have decided to study like mad, just to prove that it is true. When I told my mother I wouldn't be helping to bring money home anymore because I had to study, she was stunned. She had wanted me to quit school and I think I know why: What is the point of studying if I can't be admitted to university because my parents do not cooperate with the new regime?

Nevertheless, I am managing to catch up with the other students and to memorize the whole year's program. I have developed a keen taste for studying and for creativity. I am finally succeeding in my efforts to win over my teachers and I now have one good friend with whom I can share many things.

Together, we started to publish a newspaper which we proudly displayed on the classroom wall. Since my friend is very good in composition, she did all the writing and I handled the illustrations. At last, we could express ourselves nobly on paper. But there was one big problem – since we hadn't consulted anyone before doing this, school officials interpreted our initiative as a protest. Doesn't the new regime favour everyone equally?

Our newspaper was short-lived. One morning we walked into the classroom and found it torn to shreds. Checkmate! But this will not dampen our enthusiasm.

My friend has just been named Class President and I am put in charge of sports. Bolstered by these assignments, we eagerly start to organize various contests based on our study program. This time, our efforts are crowned with success. We also manage to organize an exciting bicycle trip for the class out in the woods where the rubber trees grow.

I have now completed ninth grade. Honorable mentions are given to the most outstanding students, based on class votes. Nobody voted for me...I know I didn't study hard in the hope of getting such honors, but just the same, I feel rejected and outraged. From this day on, I will know that the poor can never have a place in the sun nor the right to receive rewards. I resort to the only remedy I know that will ease my discontent: tears and silence...

After a good cry, I decide I want to learn all sorts of things: to play musical instruments and to weave straw mats, baskets and handbags. I also want to take art lessons and to learn how to make pottery with my hands – so calloused from chopping wood and carrying heavy loads of merchandise. I want to do everything there is an absolute madness raging in me!

Such a flurry of activity makes me dizzy. I am always behind in my payments for these courses and I end up selling my books and mandolin. Such wasted efforts to improve my lot and take my revenge on life and on this heartless society! I want them to give me a chance to discover the world, the whole universe with my own bare hands and with my own eyes. But nobody sees me as I am. People only see me as the "daughter of a fool", whose family is poor and ragged. We are scorned by our neighbours and rejected even by our own relatives.

CHAPTER 6

THE DREAM

One day I was shaken out of my stupor – out of my dream to become a somebody – when Mother said to me, "You and your brother Thanh will be leaving Vietnam soon on a boat." I was totally speechless. An adventure on a boat? I never dreamed of that! I had noticed before that certain people we knew had suddenly disappeared. It is said that they tried to flee the country in fishing boats. Some managed to find freedom, while others found rest at the bottom of the sea. Even worse, their escapes sometimes lead to prison, forced labour camps and no freedom at all.

Anyway, only rich people can afford a place on those fishing boats. How can I possibly take such a risk without any money? But my mother did say, "You'll be leaving...yes, you will leave..." Me, crawl out of my cocoon to live like a butterfly, free to fly up in the sky and be admired as one of God's marvelous creatures? I can't find the words to express my joy. Yet, life has taught me to be wary of happiness, that way I won't be too disappointed when the happiness goes away.

I start building dreams but soon shatter them, one by one, for they are nothing but illusions. Indifference seems to be the best attitude to adopt. Impassively, I ask my mother how she plans to pay for our fares. She explains that she has saved enough to buy one ounce of gold and that Grandmother also lent her some. At first, she had wanted to send only my brother so that he might avoid conscription. Then, by mere chance, she met a gentleman who owns a fishing boat. He is willing to take my brother with him for two ounces of gold and I can go along too if she promises to give two more ounces later.

Many people pay up to ten ounces of gold to leave. Good fortune seems to be coming my way at last. We don't even have enough money for food, yet here we are planning a voyage to freedom. This must be why Mother prays so much and attends mass every morning. In silence and prayer, she has been planning this escape. Sometimes I find it hard to understand how Christ can remain at the heart of a family as tormented as ours and where everything is in shambles.

Mother often looks at me with her weary but tender eyes. For some time now, her constant struggle for survival has created a void between us. Today, her eyes seem to bridge the gap. Her words to us sound like a dying person's last wishes, "You're older than your brother", she says to me, "so I entrust him to you. Take good care of him, both physically and morally. If anything should happen, put your trust in God. Never forget the purpose of this voyage. You will be alone in a foreign land, perhaps living in comfort, but never forget who you are. Fulfill your obligations as Christians, as brother and sister, as citizens and students. You love to study and you must continue to do so; it is the only thing that will save you from a life of misery. And now," she concludes, "you must be very discreet. Nobody must know about your departure, not even your father. The walls have ears and, unfortunately, a tongue."

Thanh, who is in grade eight, goes to school in the morning, whereas I go in the afternoon now. In our spare time, he repairs bicycles for my mother's shop while I check the inventory and order whatever we need. Then I do my homework, or rather practice my favourite sport: tackling books filled with numbers.

Occasionally, my brother will ask me to help him with his assignments in mathematics and science. I am always more than pleased to give him a lesson. I love to play big sister, but Thanh refuses to obey me. Despite the fact that our interests are markedly different, we are very fond of each other. Extremely protective of one another, we would never let anyone hurt the other. Now that we know we will be alone to face the storms ahead, our fraternal bonds are even stronger. Together, we will manage on our own, just like we did when we were young and our parents both worked. Alone at home, we had to take on responsibilities: wash ourselves, lift a bench, answer the door, nurse a bruise...But now we are fourteen and fifteen; we have grown up and changed and so have our problems. The thought of our imminent departure has brought back these childhood memories.

The new school where I am now completing grade ten leaves me cold because I adore studying and reading by myself. Although it is the largest in the city, this school has no library, no laboratories. There are often more than fifty students in a class, yet only a few of them take their studies seriously. Others, whose motivation and interest have been dashed by the thought of conscription, only dream of ways to escape from this labyrinth. Even the teachers' reprimands and threats cannot dissipate the apathy which prevails amongst us. We feel lost and abandoned for the professors themselves are afraid to speak truthfully about the purpose of our studies. Our future looks gloomy. We refuse to blindly obey orders. We want to know why. I can't blame the teachers. They are also victims of the system. That is why I prefer to learn things on my own.

Although the future seems uncertain, I try to add a little 'zing' to my life as a student. Instead of attending a boring history course, I switch to a physics class by changing my name. Sometimes I give stupid answers just for laughs, and I get thrown out of the classroom. But what I enjoy doing most is wandering out into the fields behind the school while my classmates sit listening to a literature or political science teacher. All these subjects harp on the same themes: love for your Country, for the People, for the Regime; gratitude and praise for the Pioneers of the Revolution and for its Leaders; and on a philosophy which denies the existence of a supreme being. It is pointless to talk about love, freedom and independence when none of these ideals exist around us. Strolling across the fields, I sometimes meet others who find nature more appealing than school.

At exam time, I do quite well in mathematics and science. But in the other subjects, I cheat in every way I can. I know it is not an honourable thing to do, but I do it anyway, just for the fun of it, just to spite my teacher and to get my revenge. Luckily, I have never been caught.

It is now early November 1979. For some inexplicable reason, our departure has been delayed. Occasionally, I show up at school for the last class. Since everyone is used to seeing me appear and disappear, nobody suspects anything. It is very important that I be discreet so as not to jeopardize our plan. Impatiently, I await the departure day, hoping and praying that it is not just a dream.

My mother has great confidence in this boat-owner's family who she knows. Today a lady comes to bring us news. Her name is Madame Le Du. She looks like a very kind and honest person; so does her husband. They sell used bicycle and motorcycle parts in our neighbourhood also. Little by little, I start to piece the story together: the boat on which we will be leaving belongs to their son-in-law. Madame Le Du is only letting her sons leave with us. Personally, I feel reassured, but my brother doesn't show any emotion. I can't tell if he is worried about the trip because he doesn't say a word.

CHAPTER 7

DEPARTURE

At last, the time has come! Madame Le Du is here to take us to her house. Kneeling in front of a picture of Jesus and Mary, we say a final prayer with Mother whose eyes are brimming with tears. In a halting voice, she begs us to not to forget our heritage. My baby brother and sisters seem to sense what is going on. They remain silent and sad. Luckily, Father isn't home. He usually roams around town all day, straddling his bicycle like a lone horseman riding off in the wind. This morning, he might be down the road somewhere, weighing the pros and cons of a problem; a smile or grimace expresses his approval or dissatisfaction with the conclusion.

After wiping away her tears, Mother's smile returns. We leave without having seen our father, without kissing Mother good-bye and without saying a word to the children. Only our eyes exchange a farewell glance. I take one last sweeping look at our house, our home and loved ones. Oh, home! The hands of fate have made me break my promise to you. Today I must leave you, perhaps forever. And I hasten outside so I won't hear her rebuffs.

Cautious and silent, my brother and I head down the street behind Madame Le Du who is walking ahead of us. We don't want to arouse any suspicions. Thanh is going so fast I can hardly keep up with him. I feel as light as a feather. We are setting out on the adventure of our lives with no luggage, no money, nothing but the light clothes on our backs and our hearts bursting with joy. The pains of separation are already weakening.

The streets are bustling with cyclists and pedestrians, but none of them know the excitement I feel inside. My whole being is attuned to the action around me and my head is bobbing in every direction. I experience a shock as we pass by one of my friend's houses. Many of my classmates live on this street and I don't want to meet them now. It would only complicate matters.

Lost in my own reverie, I try to forget the long road ahead. With a start, I come to a stop when a certain date comes flashing through my mind: today is November 11th. Why is it important? Tomorrow I am supposed to write the regional examination that will determine my educational future. Snapping out of my daze, I suddenly realize I have been standing here on the sidewalk for some time. Thanh is far ahead of me, so I have to run to catch up with him and together we continue to play follow-the-leader.

Madame Le Du is still guiding us along. We left home about twenty minutes ago and, after making countless detours, we finally arrive at her house. Everything is ready, so we immediately leave again with her eldest son, Le Du, whom I have already met, and his twenty-year old friend, Tuê. All four of us take a bus, then a minibus, and finally a taxi. We change directions so often that I am completely lost. But I trust these men implicitly. Now we are walking in the heart of the city. Le Du suggests we stop and have dinner. I find myself inside a small restaurant which simply appeared out of nowhere. Faced with a steaming bowl of soup, I tell them I am not hungry.

"Eat", Le Du says, "because this will be the last Vietnamese food you'll taste." If it is to be the last, then I want to gobble up everything in sight, and more – this sky, this street, these faces and the expressions of my people. Yes, I want to feast my eyes and swallow everything around me to appease my hunger one last time!

Once again, we are on the run. On an unfamiliar street, we stop and enter a café where we just sit and wait. But what are we waiting for? I don't know and our friends don't bother explaining anything. They just quietly sit there smoking and drinking coffee. It is so mysterious! I don't even dare ask where we are. I glance over at my brother and note that, like me, he is calmly sipping his lemonade, acting like everyone else. Time drags on endlessly...Just when I have finished my drink, a man comes over to our table to talk to Le Du, but I can't hear what they are saying.

After he leaves, we walk out of the café and board a minibus. Through the window, I watch the trees and houses gradually fade away behind us in a haze of uncertainty. I feel sad and lonely thinking about my mother and wondering what she is doing now. Is she thinking of us? What is going to happen to us?

Once more we stop in some unfamiliar spot. We end up sitting and waiting in another café. I still don't know what we are waiting for. Seeing everyone so tense, Tuê tries to make us laugh and he succeeds because his stories are really funny. But after a short while, we each withdraw into our own private thoughts and dreams. So many questions remain unanswered: When will we leave? Which way are we going? Will we manage to escape? What will happen during the voyage? I find it very strange that I have not seen any water, yet we are supposed to be leaving by boat.We try to fill the time with a bit of small talk so that we don't look too conspicuous. And I have no idea what time it is because time seems to have stopped. As soon as we have finished our drinks, we switch to yet another restaurant. Another lemonade...I never drank so much of it. Hardly anyone is here. We drink and wait...again. When will the curtain rise and let the action begin?

Twilight slowly folds away and fades into darkness over every rooftop. After a time, I can hear the news coming from the nearby houses so it must be around ten or eleven o'clock. Finally, Le Du gets up, commanding us to follow him. I am so happy to be on the move again. Without rushing, he crosses the street then disappears down a dark alley. We follow. I am afraid because I can't see a thing. Only the sound of footsteps ahead guide me. Although trembling with fear, I feel like laughing because we look like silly kids playing hide-and-seek in the streets at night.

At last I can hear the lapping waves nearby. I am so excited: Now I know it isn't a dream. Suddenly, someone grabs me by the shoulder and pushes me towards the right. I can just barely see the outline of several covered boats rocking to and fro. Somebody, whose face I can't make out, stretches out a hand to help me board one of the boats. It is so dark that I bump my leg on something. Everyone is perfectly silent during all this time – like in a spy movie!

Here we are crouched down and packed like sardines. When I softly call out my brother's name...no reply. A gentle voice tells me, "Don't worry, Thanh is on board. He got on ahead of me." It is Tuê who is sitting next to me. Now I feel reassured.

The engine suddenly starts piercing the still of the night. The police will surely hear the noise and come chasing after us. The idea of prison chills my bones.

From the glow of the city lights on the water, I can see that we are being pulled by another boat. Its engine is sputtering and I doubt it can take us to America. I don't even know where America is, only that it is far, far away...When I spoke about this to Tuê, the engine was making so much noise I could hardly hear his reply. He said we were supposed to rendezvous with a bigger boat which would take us across the ocean. It is beginning to sink in just how difficult and dangerous my 'adventure' is really going to be. But ordinary people can be courageous too, can't they?

The two boats sway to the roaring tune of the engine, making us dizzy. I feel nauseous. When the lady next to me vomits at my feet, I can't help but do the same. Others follow suit as our vessels forge ahead into the darkness, oblivious to our woes. I can't wait to get out of here!

Finally, we reach the rendezvous point at the mouth of the river. But only the wind and rippling wavelets are there to greet us. The big boat didn't come. So we wait. Did it have a mishap? Everybody is worried and wondering what to do. When a child starts to cry, the situation becomes even more dramatic. Although the engine is off, the boat continues its unruly dance and swaying motion. I still feel sick even though my stomach is empty. Right now, I am more concerned about sea-sickness than about the outcome of our voyage.

After waiting almost an hour, the men decide to turn back. The big boat was delayed by something or someone. Maybe the police found out...? It is very dangerous to remain here any longer. When the boats head back to shore, I feel devastated. I'm drawn into a black void where my thoughts have no more meaning. Lord, don't you want us to leave? Maybe in your divine plan I still have things to do at home? Well, my Master, thy will be done. Yes, thy will be done...The words so often spoken by my mother blindly echo in my mind.

Cras-s-sh! Everyone is startled to attention by a terrifying noise and jolt. Before I can figure out what is happening, a woman sitting aft of the boat, with a child in her arms, falls overboard. A man dives in to rescue them. All the passengers start panicking, causing the boat to pitch dangerously. I suddenly realize why it is no longer so dark in here: the roof is gone. It has been ripped off. Overhead, an eerie shadow looms over us like a giant arm – it is a bridge.

Everybody is climbing out and running up to the bridge. When I realize the boat is practically empty, my heart starts pounding. I try to get up but my legs are too numb. Voices call out my name: it is Le Du, Tuê and Thanh. "Yes, I'm here", I reply, struggling to get out but the men have to help me. Le Du gently scolds me for dallying. I am still dumbfounded by what has happened. The police must have heard the noise of the accident because we hear gunshots in the distance. Le Du begs us to hurry. We dash off in two separate groups: Le Du and Thanh go first, Tuê and I follow.

We are walking fast, very fast; practically running towards the distant glow of civilization. Le Du seems to know where he is going. Avoiding the highway, we head down a muddy road where our feet soon become heavy with clay. I take giant steps, trying to advance as quickly as possible. Wide open fields stretch out on either side of the road. I am scared and I also feel sorry for all of us.

We are not thieves, yet here we are running from the light of justice like bandits! I think I know what caused the accident: before reaching the mouth of the river, I noticed we had gone under a bridge. When we returned at high tide, there wasn't enough room for the boats to slip under it. That is why we are here, walking barefoot beneath this dark sky whose eyes are hidden behind heavy clouds of gray, refusing to see us.

Thanh and Le Du are walking incredibly fast. Once in a while, they look back to make sure we were still following. Tuê drags me by the hand like a child. When I was young, my father would hold my hand like this, and I would feel secure and trusting. During this trek with Tuê, I gradually regain my confidence. It gives my legs strength and sharpens my vision. Being the eldest at home, my role as group leader did not allow me to pass on my responsibilities to anyone. Now I just have to follow. My destiny is linked to all these people who are lost in the night.

In this eerie darkness and treacherous silence, I think of the long journey made by the Jews of yesteryear. But we are certainly not heading for the Promised Land. No. We are returning to a place of eternal darkness to dream of only one thing: escape!

Have we been walking for two, four or five hours? I have no idea. It is almost daylight and we have reached a village where people are getting ready to go to work. It must be around four o'clock. Le Du enquires where we can find a wharf, explaining that we have had an accident with our boat. From our clothing and manners, the villagers can easily guess that we are from the city. I really can't judge if their reaction to us is one of sympathy or suspicion. As we walk through the village, I find the stares very intimidating and I hope and pray they won't find out about our escape plan. Luckily, we have no luggage.

We reach the dock just in time to board a scow already jam-packed with people. Having to sit close to the edge, I almost fall overboard. Tuê smiles and says I should lean on a lady's luggage, which I timidly proceed to do. The lady smiles and seems honoured to do me this favour. What a relief I feel when the scow gets under way. Somehow, things haven't turned out too badly. Using the last bit of money in his pocket, Le Du pays for our tickets.

When we arrive at the landing dock, we notice a bus stop nearby. But first we head for the water's edge to wash up. We look terrible. In this giant swaying mirror, I see the reflection of a clown: short, tousled hair, mud-spotted clothes and wet slacks clinging to my weary legs. As I bend down to remove the dirt between my toes I think, "What am I doing here by this unfamiliar river, in the midst of an indifferent crowd?" There must be an explanation but I prefer to enjoy the bliss of ignorance. Questions are more soothing than answers.

A few minutes later, we climb on a bus which is just about to leave. Our diplomat, Le Du, manages to borrow money from a young girl who was also a passenger on the scow. Bouncing joyfully away from the stoney parking lot, the bus then gently rolls down the highway. Le Du and Tuê are talking with the girl from whom they borrowed our fares. They look like their old selves again: their smiles, courteous manners and sense of humour seem to have returned.

My brother and I are sitting in the front seat, as mute as two frightened rabbits being driven to the marketplace. I am cold and the chilling drafts make me shiver. Once again, as I glance over at Thanh, I feel that strong undefinable bond that unites us. "Are you cold?" I ask and he shakes his head.

We have nothing to say to each other. It is true that we never really learned to talk to one other except to discuss math problems or to argue over an explanation of a phenomenon in physics. I feel so alone and I think he does too. Since one is as handicapped as the other in this respect, we withdraw into our separate shells.

The bus is moving like a straight and speedy arrow. The window of the bus acts as a screen on which a nature film is projected and narrated by the wind: boundless rice fields, lush green carpets rolling out as far as the eye can see, timid gardens hiding behind their bamboo fences, pretty houses with thatched roofs and finally, the center of town.

When the bus comes to a stop, everybody gets off. I am moving like a robot and my head feels like lead. We board another bus, and fifteen minutes later, we get off on a very familiar street: It is the one where my school is located. Today is Wednesday and my classmates are waiting near the entrance. When I stop one of the boys to ask for information concerning the examination, he looks at me from head to toe while he answers. Seeing a questioning look in his eyes, I quickly walk away to join the others. I notice that Le Du is no longer with us as we make our way to his mother's house. I feel so embarrassed to be seen walking down the street like this – barefoot and dirty.

When we arrive at Madame Le Du's, my mother is already there. She had heard the news and is overjoyed to see us, safe and sound. I too am happy to see her again, yet I am sorry our escape attempt failed. My mother asks if we were afraid. After glancing at Thanh, I say "no". She thanks Tuê and Madame Le Du for acting as our guides. Le Du smiles, but his mother looks worried because her boys were on the big boat which was supposed to pick us up and she still hasn't had any news from them.

On our way home, Mother tells us that Father still knows nothing. She simply told him we had gone to visit our aunt for a few days. I am still thinking about the voyage and I am choked up with discontentment and disappointment. Unable to concentrate on what my mother is saying, I have to bite my lips in order to stem the flow of tears welling up in my eyes. I feel like a child from whom a gift has been taken away without any explanation. But now I must try to be reasonable; it is all over. It was only a dream, an illusion, a mirage. I must be destined to live in this country where I shed my first tears and probably where I will also draw my last breath.

CHAPTER 8

AND LIFE GOES ON

As time goes by, I am fighting a constant battle with myself, struggling to control my anger, my laziness and my pride.

At home, Father sits motionless in a chair, keeping watch over the empty shop. His eyes are fixed on the street and an eternal smile adorns his face. When I arrive, I simply say "Papa" and smile at him. That's all. I prefer not to add anything else in order to avoid any complications.

He looks well today. Without changing his composure, he asks why we came back so soon. Confused by his question, I don't know what to answer. Luckily, Mother comes to the rescue, explaining that we missed the bus. He asks no further qustions. And life goes on as if nothing happened.

It is almost noon and time for lunch; I am hungry and not the least bit tired. My exam is at twelve-thirty, so I have to rush. After showering, I borrow my brother's trousers, my sister's blouse and my mother's sandals. Then I grab a pen and a sheaf of papers, hop on my bike and dash off as quickly as I can.

At school, it is the same routine: lock up my bike, run up the stairs at the sound of the bell, and finally, face that big blackboard as black as the night I have just spent. The teacher slowly writes out the exam questions on the board. As we sit and wait for him to finish, I listen to the screeching sounds of chalk-on-slate. That blackboard has taught me many things over the years, yet it never talks. Is that wisdom? If so, then it is the only one who is wise because I need to talk, to tell stories, to discuss, to shout, to howl with rage, to destroy... But so far I have only done it through silence and tears.

The teacher's voice interrupts my thoughts. I don't quite understand what he is saying. I read the questions, get ready to write but I don't know where to start. So I read them over a second time, then a third, but the more I read the exam, the longer and more complicated it seems. I write and erase constantly, which doesn't get me anywhere. I feel as though my brain has been dulled. Although totally dissatisfied, I manage to hand in my exam. Later, out in the hallway, when I compare my answers with those of the other students, I am shattered. Theirs aren't at all the same as mine.

Days and months go by. Nothing has changed: people continue to kow-tow like frightened puppies before the mighty and growl like roaring lions at the meek and poor.

Everything and everyone is subjected to strict controls. Any excuse is a valid reason to threaten cutting our rations of rice or vegetables; rallies are compulsory for people of all ages. We often have to march down the streets, not as strikers or dissidents but as participants in demonstrations organized by the District Committee or by the school authorities.

In school, we learn the theories of Marx and Lenin. I like their ideology but it is frustrating to compare theory and reality! Isn't it too idealistic to expect equality for one and all? They have destroyed the former monetary system and established a new one in order to give a specific amount of money to every family. Yet we are poorer than ever. Where are the people who govern this country?

How can we talk of justice in a country where there are no more lawyers, no more judges? I never hear anyone talk about trials. People mysteriously disappear. My uncle has been in a labour camp since 1975. He was so kind and gentle with us. I really don't understand all this...it is all so confusing!

We are kept ignorant of the laws and human rights of our country and also of its political structure. When I was in grade four, we were taught about these things. But now...ignorance, yes ignorance...is my most serious handicap. I don't know if I can trust this government, this socialist regime which is leading us to communism. But only 'fools' can voice their opinions without fearing for their lives.

Once we reach the point where we can no longer speak our minds without fear of reprisal, how can we talk of freedom? Yet our country's motto is: Independence, Freedom, Happiness. I think I have to know about other countries to see if this is true. But because all the information is controlled by the government, how can I possibly find out?

Freedom! Who are you that politicians should proclaim you so? I don't know what you are, but when they talk about you, our leaders say: "It is better to die for freedom than to live like slaves." Many a Vietnamese have taken these words literally by fleeing the country and risking death in order to find you.

Talking about happiness now seems pointless to me. My family and I spend all our waking hours in search of a piece of bread to feed ourselves. We laugh, we cry, we eat, we sleep, we work, and we count our pennies but we never say, "I'm happy."

The victims of the last war and of the new regime, who are now physically or mentally scarred, have but one pitiful trade: they are beggars! Never has there been so much distrust between neighbours, between parents and children, between brothers and sisters. There is no more charity or human compassion in this society of ours. My heart bleeds from so many painful experiences.

One day my father, tried to hang himself with a rope in front of the house while Mother was at the back in the kitchen. The children were screaming and crying "Maman!" while the neighbours looked on as though we were puppets in a circus, or wild little monkeys jumping around a sad clown. My mother rushed out, asking for help. The people came forward but only to scoff at us even more. We were alone to help her. Thank God, Father was saved, but I realized then that we are always alone.

Yes, that's how life goes on, without mercy or compassion. Family squabbles have no season. While my father worries about the future of our country and flies into a rage over one abstract issue or another, my mother faces the daily problem of getting us our next meal. My sisters cry when they leave for school with a pair of torn slacks or an empty ink bottle.

We are fighting a losing battle with scabies and lice. I often dream of having lots of money to cure my father, to allow my mother to rest, and to pay for my brothers' and sisters' schooling. It hurts to feel so helpless.

Each morning, the crowing rooster reminds me that it is time to pray. The road leading to church is as dark as my future. All the street lights are smashed and those in my heart are turned off. I am so afraid of the dark.

Every night when the sun goes down, I think of death. In silence, daylight withdraws and the sun's youthful power withers. Alas, everything comes to an end. I haven't accomplished anything; life can't possibly stop here! If the days feel oppressive, the nights seem even more so.

Suddenly it is spring again – I will be leaving

CHAPTER 9

RENEWED HOPE

Yes, it is true, really true! Madame Le Du came back. I find her smiling face so beautiful. She says the big boat came back without any problem and another trip is being organized on this very boat. She is like the fairy godmother in the stories my mother used to tell us; she has touched my life with her magic wand again! Although it is December, it feels like spring. I can see flower buds soaking up the morning dew and swallows flying in the sunlight. I am no longer hungry. I only thirst for freedom across the waves!

This time I know we will make it. The fiasco of our last attempt is now a fading memory and I am filled with renewed energy and hope. In the evening, I start studying again and helping my brothers and sisters with their homework. I pass all my Christmas exams and get the highest mark in literature. It is both fantastic and catastrophic because I am slowly becoming a communist, unknowingly. For one thing, in my compositions I have been glorifying the communist contradiction. It is time for me to put an end to this game before I sell my soul to socialist zealots...

Christmas is here. My sister Ly isn't playing the role of Santa this year because Mother has nothing to put in her bag.

We are not going to act out the Nativity scene because there is so much else to do and to think about. Christmas is no longer important enough to be mentioned on television, on the radio or at school. The only place where the birth of Christ is quietly celebrated is in our parish church and at home.

Although everything has changed, there is one thing that makes me happy. For the first time in five years, Father is well at Christmas! He gets dressed and comes to mass with us without getting angry or making a scene. When the angelic voices of the choir ring out joyfully, I feel my cold heart melt. The peaceful, loving atmosphere in which the newborn child is welcomed gives me renewed confidence and hope. I have good reason to pray: my upcoming voyage.

After mass, we walk up to the manger, and the children's eyes fill with wonder. For us, the birth of Christ is as fascinating a story as the "ArabianNights" with all its mystery! Everybody looks happy! Oh, how I love my brothers and sisters.

Back at home, Mother has prepared steaming bowls of soup for the midnight feast. She watches us eat with a rare smile on her face. But this Christmas Eve, everyone is smiling, laughing, and playing. There is a contagious feeling of merriment in the air. Just as we finish our soup, the lights go off. The government regularly cuts off the city power supply one day a week, in order to save electricity. Is it coincidence that they choose tonight?

Since it is Christmas, I try to forget these frustrations and to make the best of this happy day with my family. While Mother puts away the dishes, she tells me she has been praying very hard for our trip. I tell her that I have also been praying. After a while, she leaves the house with my youngest brother to go and visit my grandmother. I realize suddenly that I didn't wish anybody a "Merry Christmas".

Over the past few years, many Christmas customs have been dropped but this night, in the candle glow, Kim and I start tuning our violins. Together, we play "Silent Night" and "Jingle Bells". The others join in, singing. With their hands,

Thanh and Ly drum out the beat on the table. Harmony is essential to happiness!

The dark streets beckon. All the children love to go galloping so out we go, down the street. I am just walking along, softly whistling Christmas tunes. And Christmas is already over!

Another day goes by and nothing happens. The laws of the universe are changeless. With its chilling, wintery humour, nature waits for spring. As for me, I wait for that final day when my new adventure will begin.

Rain or shine, I keep up with all my extra curricular activities as though I only had another month to live. I don't have a minute's rest. Whenever I am too tired to practice my music, I do geometry or read for a while. I find it extremely gratifying to help my sisters, and brothers with their homework. Every day I have to pedal for miles and miles to attend my courses or to take my sisters to school.

I can't control myself and yet I don't even have enough money to pay for my lessons or books. Only the voyage...or death can stop me...

I am starting to feel weak and chilled and my belly aches. Seeing me in such a pitiful state, Mother is quite worried and she starts scolding me for not having listened to her. When she starts to cry, Father also scolds me. But he is not as worried because he doesn't know what is at stake; he knows nothing about our upcoming departure.

The doctor comes to examine me and declares that I have typhoid fever. He questions my mother about what I ate the previous night, then recommends a liquid diet. His austere look scares me. He jabs a needle in me, and it hurts when I lie down. I am so afraid to die and I truly regret all my foolishness. Lying here in bed, drained of all energy, I am afraid to fall asleep in case I never wake up.

In my semi-conscious state, I hear a voice. It is Madame Le Du saying to my mother, "The boat will leave in a few days." Now I must go to sleep and dream, because I want to get better quickly. The joy of knowing I will be leaving soon helps me sleep and dream. Here I am, out on the ocean, sitting in a big boat slicing through the waves like a scissor blade. I ask the man sitting next to me if we will soon be arriving. With a smile and pointing to hazy gray spots out on the horizon he says, "America will greet us with open arms in twenty four hours, my dear."

When I wake up the next morning, my body feels refreshed and my mind is at peace. I don't know how many days I have been drifting in and out of sleep but before crawling out of bed this morning, I say the prayer my mother taught us.

Madame Le Du's visit was not a dream. She had come to say we would be leaving Tuesday, January 22, 1980. Out of her meagre savings, Mother gave her two hundred dollars for our provision of dried food.

I really trust this lady but still, fear gnaws at me. Mother tells me to rest now because I must be well and strong for the voyage. Alone, in bed, I ponder over my activities which were suddenly interrupted five days ago. I have no regrets, because these past few days of prayer, meditation, rest and daydreaming have done me a world of good. But when I think of those who are studying and working while I am idle, I become anxious to resume my normal life. "Studying is like swimming against the stream; if you don't keep it up, you experience a setback."

Now my day has officially started. Both my sisters are already up; their places in bed are already cold. They left the netting open and five or six fat mosquitoes, too heavy to fly away, are nestling there.

In less than a minute, I make my bed – which means folding the mosquito netting and the blankets, and rolling up the matting (my sister Ly didn't wet the bed last night!). After jumping off the bed, I softly walk to over the window. Somehow the air outside smells different today. It must be purified by the sound of the bells and hymns coming from St. Thomas Church and blessed by the solemn gestures of the old Dominican priest early this morning.

I have a strong feeling that something both great and tragic is about to happen to me. It is as though...a part of myself was slowly dying...this death is not so terrible. It is gentle and invisible. Every puff of this blessed air I breathe seeps through my body.

This attic, as colorless as the rags of a beggar, enfolds me and pushes me towards the window. Here, rusty iron bars stripe the sky, and its brightness is dimmed by filtering cobwebs. Even though this window frame is not made of shiny wood with a marble sill or adorned with transparent glass and flowered curtains – like at my godfather's house, I prefer it because my father built it. It is my very own...it frames my life. Through it, enter the joyously resounding sounds of church bells and those more plaintive and deep from the Buddhist temple. Beyond the iron bars and cobwebs and beyond the rooftops, lies a peaceful cemetery like a flowery bedspread which is never pulled down. In a hundred years from now, who will fret over my sleep in this room or remember this window of mine? Only the sun will come around to wake up the birds and flowers without disturbing the weary dust of life to which our bodies will return...

Mother is back from mass and is opening up the shop. I go downstairs and give her a hand to take out and dust off the last few bicycle parts left to sell, trying to think of something to say. Finally, I ask if she went to mass. I feel stupid because I already know the answer. She adds that Papa also went and he hasn't returned yet. I tell her I will go to four o'clock mass. My brothers and sisters are having breakfast before going to the nine o'clock service, except Ly who has already left the house with her friends (her gang of hooligans, my mother says). She asks me how I feel and seems pleased with my reply. Peering outside, she says she hopes Tuesday will be a nice sunny day like today, with the sidewalks filled with people strolling about. I leave her to go and take a shower.

Because of the fever, I haven't taken one all week. Groping in the dark corner where an enormous pile of washing is lying, I look for my clothes. The things we wear are so tattered, we children do not think it worth the effort to fold them neatly. Mother, however, is always asking us to restore some order in that corner. Oh, I am so furious! Ly took off with my slacks, leaving me hers with a rip in the seat and a torn cuff. Now I have to mend them before I take my shower; otherwise I have nothing to wear. Just wait till she comes home. I will give her a piece of mind!!!

The cold water washes away all my belligerent intentions. I whistle a tune while I am dressing. When I go down to the kitchen, Mother points to a pot where my breakfast awaits me. All that remains is a thick layer of half-burnt rice with an empty box of brown sugar! Seeing the look on my face, she tries to comfort me by saying she will prepare lunch a bit earlier. So I have to be content with my "grain" of rice and salt.

Partly because of the intense heat today, the only strollers on the street, are soldiers in their green uniforms. I am not afraid of them. On the contrary, we make good money from them. They are our best customers for bicycle parts. Those I fear most wear a yellow uniform: policemen! They carry long rifles and revolvers and they are always chasing after me when I try to sell my goods on the street. Here they come again. Quickly I dash in, carrying boxes of spokes, handlebars and tires which were out on the sidewalk.

Mother, who was busy washing out a tiny box, is startled by my actions. But when she sees the two jaundiced silhouettes walk by, she immediately understands. Then, turning back to her little box, she says, as if to herself, "They came this week (meaning the government officials and the police) to talk about taxes. Do you know what I told them? I said: Ladies, Gentlemen, I have a sick husband and seven children to feed and I haven't made a cent for days. If the government needs my taxes so badly, they can come and get my parts that are rusting away for lack of customers. They answered that they had only come to make an estimate and that they would be back." As I listen to her, I have to smile for there is something so stubborn and naive about her attitude.

She keeps looking at this tiny box. Pointing to it, she says it will be filled with Eucharistic bread for us to take along on the boat. Now I know why she prepared it with so much love and care. When I ask her where she will get it, she answers "Grandma will ask the parish priest for some." She then leaves me in charge of the shop and walks over to my grandmother's house. It is a good thing my baby brother is not home (he is at church with the others) because he usually follows her everywhere. Although he is five now, it wasn't very long ago that Mother stopped breast-feeding him.

The house doesn't remain quiet very long. It is already ten o'clock and the children are back from church. Thanh quickly changes into his shorts to go and play soccer with his friends. He runs out as if the house were on fire, while my sisters and the baby settle down on the floor with scissors and paper, cutting out paper dolls.

It is a quiet, uneventful Sunday, as usual. Several merchants walk by, looking around and chatting, as always, I greet them with a smile, but my innocuous words mask my hypocritical thoughts and revolt. Reality is too cruel and mediocre. Reality scares me because it makes my notions of love and happiness seem vulgar and ridiculous. It shatters my most precious visions of life. Sitting here like a buddhist monk, I can feel the pulse of life beating faster, stronger and more regularly than my own heart...shuffling feet, screeching tires, children's laughter, chattering neighbours, itinerant merchants calling out. Reality reminds each living cell that death is at hand...my howling conscience tells me to react but does not tell me what I must do. I just sit here.

This evening during mass, I am unable to pray. I simply gaze at the statues. God knows who I am and He will surely inspire me. After the final blessing, I walk out to the church yard. It is here that my parents first met and I have come here, to mend my broken heart. I let the sun leave these grounds before me because I am tired of having to run before the wind. The last rays of dusk nudge my shoulder, beckoning me. For a minute, the tempting city lights sparkle in my eyes, but the shadows of darkness rivet my feet to the ground. Everything looks bigger, more imposing in the dark. It gives me the shivers. The church bells which earlier rang out as a joyful trio now whimper softly. The statue of the Blessed Virgin reigns over all things. Even with my eyes closed, I still see and feel her penetrating gaze upon me. From her outstretched hands seem to flow the peaceful blue waters of the

Pacific – like the peace which I will soon know! With this glimmer of hope in mind, I smile up at Mary. Leaving the shadows behind, I head for the city of lights where my vision of things will not be so clear. But behind me, I can feel the embrace of her loving eyes.

As I pedal down the road, I feel happy and unchained. I want to shout my final words to this indifferent city, "I am going to be free – free as a bird!"

I know that what I am about to do is crazy, but I must take the risk. So many thoughts are churning in my brain that I have to do something to numb the pains of waiting. I make a dash to my friend Nhan's house. Face to face, without a word of greeting, I can tell she is worried, tired and sad. Yet, we stand there together, near my bike, for hours and talk, punctuating our sentences with sighs. When we bid each other farewell, it seems like the world is breaking in two so that we can each have a half.

The door is locked and the lights are out when I finally get home. It must be quite late because the "midnight masquerade" is over. The smell of perfume with a blend of cigar odor still lingers in the air. Trembling, I knock on the door and the silence which solidly barred the entrance is broken as my father speaks. "Where have you been?" Without a word and bowing my head, I go into the house. Mother whispers a few harsh words and I know she is very angry. To ease my fear, I run up to the attic and immediately say my prayers. I crawl into bed next to Kim who is sleeping like an angel. Ly hasn't come home yet. She is even braver than I.

The following afternoon at five-thirty, the gentle peal of the school bell reminds me that my liberation is near. I am happy to have yet another day pass; time is like a mortal enemy to me. I run down the stairs from the third floor of my school to the parking lot. Lost in my own thoughts, I open and close my bicycle lock twice. Two boys standing nearby seem to be having problems too. Out of curiosity, I look over and recognize them from my class. One says to the other, pointing at me: "Are you sure she is a girl?"

58

Author's family including Keo the pet dog, together in Vietnam for the last time.

Doan's mother at twenty-two.

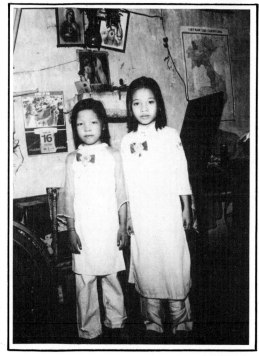

Sisters Kim and Mai wearing first communion costume just before Doan's first escape attempt.

Author's four sisters and the small brother she left behind in Vietnam. Photo taken at Saigon Zoo shortly after Doan's escape.

Vietnamese refugees in barracks similar to the one Doan and Thanh lived in for three months in Indonesia. One hundred and twenty people crowded into each barrack room and were alloted 9 square feet of living space per person. Many lived in these conditions for two years or more.

uneral of Doan's maternal grandmother. White band around forehead is traditional Vietnamese mourning
ostume. Buddist temple and bicycle shop is in background. Author's home out of picture to right.

Author's family. Photo was taken upon receipt of the
news that Doan and Thanh were safe in Canada.
May 1980.

Author's school and teachers in front of library
that Doan wished for so much but only came after
her escape from Vietnam.

Recent picture of author Doan's Vietnam family at home in Saigon.

Doan and Thanh with new Canadian family.

It flatters me to be mistaken for a boy. But they have also touched an open wound. I know they are making fun of my appearance (rugged face and short hair). "It's none of your business!" I reply. They are stunned by my rude reaction. Looking down at their bikes, I see that the tires are completely flat. Unable to hold back a sardonic grin, I have to hurry away from the parking lot because I am going to burst out laughing at their expressions of disgust. I can see that my reputation is made.

The sun is giving nature a yellow tinge. Bay-Hien Square is flooded with light and swamped with students. What a splendid sight! As I mingle with this crowd – tomorrow's army, I feel swept along by this human tide. After a while, I leave the noisy conversations behind.

As I pedal down the street, I recognize my friend Nhan walking alongside her broken bike. I hop off and walk with her. Teasingly I say, "Either you're too heavy or the hand of vengeance is." She replies with a smirk on her face, "Neither one." I don't ask her for an explanation because we love mysteries and contradictions. We merely go on talking about the crazy things that have happened while I was sick.

Suddenly, I see my music teacher coming along on the same side of the street and I am afraid. I haven't been going to my lessons for the past three or four weeks. Stopping about three yards away from us, she smiles at me and shouts, "How come you're still here? I thought you'd be far away beneath a foreign sky by now." I can feel my tongue knotting up and my heart thumping wildly as I explain that I had been sick. But she keeps right on walking with her companion as if she hadn't heard me. I must admit that I am frightened of her, especially because of what she just said. Nhan, who knows exactly how I feel, picks up the conversation as though nothing had happened. I drop her off at the garage to have her bike repaired and go on my way. No farewell can be spoken here.

It must be almost 6:30 because the sun is playing hide-and-seek behind the trees. Shops are closing while others open up for the night. Down the street, people are rushing home. In the sky, birds flapping their wings are also heading for their nests. This could be the last time I will enjoy such a homecoming.

At home, Mother is late in closing up the shop because of last minute clients. She asks me to keep an eye on the rice that is cooking on the wood stove while she carts in the merchandise. Seeing her groping in the darkness, I try to turn on the lights for her, but she reminds me that the power was shut off to save energy. "You'll be leaving tomorrow morning," she whispers to me.

Later, while making her daily journal entries, she tells me that Madame Le Du came to confirm our departure time. A spark of joy lights up my heart, bursts into flames and flushes my cheeks when mother adds that Tuê will becoming over here tonight. I remember that he held my hand to guide me through that dark and cold night last year. My hand in his firm grasp, Tuê told me to "hang on, take courage; we must cross a plain, a village, a river and two cities before dawn. We must be faster than the sun!" I wanted to forget that night in order to live more serenely, but today, I am overjoyed to hear its beckoning whistle in the wind. That first escape attempt only heightened my taste for adventure and my desire to explore new frontiers. Lord, please don't ever ask me to forget this dream.

While we are preparing dinner, Tuê arrives. Leaving the pot of soup steaming on the fire, I follow Mother to the door. He greets her with respect and she also lets him know how happy she is to see him. He smiles at me like a big brother and asks if I am anxious to leave. Mother enquires about the boat, about food and several other things. Her face glows with tenderness. Every wrinkle reflects the gentle touch of time. Who are you, Tuê, that your message should make this woman so happy? I savour every one of their words, looks and gestures.

With some emotion, he makes this promise to my mother, "Don't worry, I will watch over them." I wish every day of my life could be a new start. We are nothing but spiders and the web of happiness we spin during our lifetime is constantly being respun and undone to fill the universe with dust.

"See you tomorrow and ...pray that all goes well!" says Tuê on his way out.

Tonight, everything is bathed in a languid atmosphere. The darkness threatens to snuff out the flickering candle. Should I worry about what is ahead or fear the slow and heavy footsteps of the unknown?

CHAPTER 10

SECOND ATTEMPT

At four-thirty, Mother wakes me up for mass. It is Tuesday, January 22nd, 1980 and the damp night forces me to button up my sweater. The world hasn't yet lifted its netting. Crowned with stars and dreams, the city sleeps like a peaceful child. As graceful and silent as a bride walking down the aisle, I pedal my way to church.

I feel quite certain we will be leaving today even though it is possible the voyage might be delayed several days...like the last time. My prayer is nothing but a painful plea, a cry for help. Up on His cross, He seems to be smiling at me. During mass, beams of sunlight accompany the old Dominican's final blessing. With one last sweeping glance, I try to record and memorize the images in my heart. Part of me will always remain here, in this peaceful haven. Tomorrow, St. Thomas Church will be nothing but a memory.

At home, I have to watch the pot of rice that is cooking while Mother and Thanh attend mass. Squatting on the floor with my chin propped up on my knees, I let the cool breeze and pleasant warmth coming from the stove gently rock me. As I sit here watching the miniature fireworks, the ashes of hidden memory are rekindled.

I remember a book of fairy tales my father gave me when I was very very young. Each spring, the good fairy, Queen of Flowers, would awaken her daughters. At the touch of her magic wand, sleeping tulips would stretch out their petals; pretty lilacs would open their eyes and exhale an exquisite scent harbored throughout winter... Startled by a piece of green wood crackling to life, I snap out of my stupor...The sun is already up. It must be close to seven o'clock. I wonder why Mother and Thanh aren't back yet. Each separation now threatens to be eternal. With clenched teeth and determined effort, I get up and start opening up the shop.

After a while mother and Thanh return, but...they are on foot. What happened? Mother tells me that somebody stole their bicycles from the church yard. A giant ball of anger threatens to choke me. How could there be so much injustice in the world? My mother's frail shoulders have a heavy enough burden to carry without any added hardships. These bicycles were part of the goods we needed to sell to pay for our trip. And now what? In this, my mother – whose wisdom and love are stronger than adversity – sees only the will of God. Father is with us, but he doesn't say a word. He seems far removed from these events, lost in a world of his own where I dare not enter, out of respect.

My mother chooses to forget about the theft and concentrate on the most important thing: our voyage. My revolt and anger in the face of this criminal catastrophe seems wicked compared to Mother's passive resignation.

Squatting on the floor in a circle (our table has been sold), the family waits for Father to say Grace before breakfast. Today, Mother adds a piece of ham to each bowl of rice – something she hasn't done in months. We all enjoy this feast, eating and chatting like we did at Grandmother's New Year's dinner, hardly aware that this is our last meal together.

As usual after breakfast, Father leaves the house. Discreetly, my sisters and baby brother are informed of our departure. What does our departure mean to them? Are we leaving forever or will we be back in a few days, like the last time? I feel as though we are being buried alive.

But who is to blame for this heart-wrenching separation? We are very sad to leave, but we would be even more miserable if we stayed together, drowning in a pool of physical and moral suffering. For the good of all, my brother and I must succeed in our escape attempt. "Grief does not put bread on your plate," Mother would often say. That is why nobody is crying; our tears flow on the inside and turn into prayers that stoke the flame of hope.

Mother calls me to the back. Wordlessly, onto my finger, she slips a gold band meticulously wrapped with thread. It is her wedding ring...the one that joined my parents and is now separating us today. Deeply moved by this gesture, I confess haltingly, "Mama, without your permission, I've taken money and spent it foolishly, I've wasted your money just to satisfy my pride. Please forgive me..." Softly she says, "You're already forgiven.

For once, I have conquered my pride...I am so happy I could die. What is this force which has given me the courage to be truthful?

My mother then calls Thanh over. Looking at both of us, she says, "I have no idea what will happen, but we have faith, so we have no reason to tremble, come what may. You are this family's only hope for the future. Life will be hard for you, as it has been for all of us lately, but God is there and He will always be your guiding light. Never forget what I am saying now and what I have already said to you. Now go in peace. God bless you. Once you reach the land of freedom, – which is our greatest hope – sell this ring and wire the money to us." She remains quite calm. She doesn't cry like the first time we left. Likewise, we are prepared to accept whatever life may hold for us...

The sidewalk area next to our place is empty; Mr. and Mrs Le Du aren't opening up their store today. Our trip isn't just a dream. Thanh is very quiet and solemn. The children just stare at us without daring to ask any questions.

Mother sends Mai – the fifth one – over to the neighbour's house to check what time it is because Father is the only one who has a watch and he is not home. She dashes out, stands outside the neighbour's door, looks at the clock, counts the hours with her index finger and runs back to say, "The little hand is at nine, the big hand is at one, and the thin one is moving too fast."

"This brings a smile to my mother's face as she turns to me saying, "Run over quickly to Grandmother's house and pick up the hosts she was getting from the parish priest!" Five minutes later I return with an empty little box. The priest would not give her any so all I can take with me from Grandmother is her smile and prayers.

Around ten o'clock, Madame Le Du arrives, putting an end to the agony of parting. One last time, Mother checks my ring and the piece of paper rolled up inside my brother's trouser cuff. It contains the address of my cousin who lives in the United States. After drinking her glass of water, Madame Le Du nonchalantly walks out of the house as though she had come on a regular visit. In turn, Thanh and I say, "I'm going, Mother!" This simple phrase, which we would always say to our parents before going out, takes on a very different meaning today. To the children, we just smile. Part of me will remain in those black, innocent eyes. But one day I will reclaim that part, I promise!

We leave the house and follow Madame's shirt tail which is flapping in the wind. Although our hands are empty, our minds are filled with memories. We leave in peace, for the young ones will preserve our childhood and complete our youthful days. Now we must go on our path like two adults. It doesn't matter where this path will lead us. What is important is to leave, and to hope.

When we finally reach Madame Le Du's house, Tuê isn't there; only Le Du and his girlfriend whom we have never met before. After a brief introduction – her name is An-Ny – we leave. I am still winded... I guess the typhoid fever has taken its toll! I ask Le Du if Mother had given him my medication and he nods in reply. After saying goodbye to his mother, all four of us walk down to Pham Hong Thai boulevard to catch a bus. My brother and I follow without even asking where we are going. Our compliance is absolute.

As we are about to board a minicar, I notice my mother in the alleyway watching and waiting. My heart wants to scream. When the vehicle starts to leave, she says, "Go in peace. I will explain everything to your father!" And she quickly disappears down the alley, hiding her grief.

We are moving so fast that the familiar surroundings soon fade away. We get off in a strange part of town and Le Du takes us to a coffee shop. Nothing new. Again we sit and wait, but for what, for whom, and why? By now we are used to this waiting game.

Frowning Le Du looks over at me and exclaims, "What is happening to your hands? They look terrible!"

"It is just dry skin peeling off. Perhaps it is because of the typhoid fever," I explain. An-Ny smiles at me, as if she understands. Then everybody grows silent. Once in a while, we make a few casual remarks so as not to attract too much attention. I am afraid that the police might show up. It is terrible to just sit and watch the time go by without knowing when it will stop and under what circumstances!

Around noon we go and eat lunch somewhere else. The sun is at its zenith, spewing its fiery rays at us like a furious god. I am blinded by the heat for a moment as we walk down the burning pavement and finally enter a Chinese restaurant. Since my brother and I aren't accustomed to eating out, we let Le Du order for us. I feel so awkward and shy that I can hardly eat my lunch. Oh, Mother, what else must we do without you?

After the meal we start walking again, and after a short distance, we meet up with Tuê on a street corner. He leads us to a sidewalk café where he introduces us to his brother, Thinh, who was already waiting for us. Then he leaves again with An-Ny. Once more, we settle down and wait. I know this area because I used to pass by here when I had to pick up my father's medicine at the hospital. I shiver when I realize we are sitting across from a police station. Tuê hasn't lost his sense of humour, but I know he is worried. So is his brother, because he doesn't talk much. While the boys chat among themselves, I have plenty of time to imagine the worst possible things that could happen to us.

It takes forever for the weather to cool down a bit. Finally Le Du comes back for us, and in Indian file we follow him through myriads of alleyways and into a house. I am scared. The house is full of strangers sitting on the floor in silence. When we enter, nobody moves. Like frightened, forelorn kittens, my brother and I crouch down in a corner, mute and paralyzed with fear. The whole house seems to be falling in on me.

Around supper time I go crawling beneath the window sills into the kitchen and ask the lady who is bathing her children for a glass of water to swallow my pills. For a minute I just stand there watching her because she is very pretty, even if there is not a hint of a smile on her face. Then I quickly rejoin my brother.

A young girl named Bich is handing out bread to everyone. She doesn't even know us; will she offer us some too, I wonder?...I am not hungry, but my brother? Remembering a scene from "Oliver Twist", I recognize in Thanh, the child for whom I shed so many tears. Who would have thought those tears would be for us, today? Yes, Bich does offer us some white and tasteless bread, as insipid as her indifferent hands. I prefer the black ration bread mother used to bring home, for it was enriched with the salty taste of her sweat and tears...This strange and listless crowd invades my privacy.

Darkness spreads her black cape over the house, spying on us through the curtains. We all move into a windowless room where a tiny light bulb spreads a sickly jaundiced glow. The hubbub of the children in this stuffy room soon dissipates by their mothers' "shushs". Again we sit and wait. As I glance around, I can't see Le Du or Tuê, but I make sure my brother is there. From now on, I know we must follow this group.

It is impossible to tell how much time goes by before we move again. Like an army of ghosts, we quietly head for the door. It is so dark that I have to make a concentrated effort to follow on the heels of the person ahead of me as we walk through a corridor, down a staircase – which I don't recall having climbed before – then across a verandah. Next we climb onto a high platform which is swaying left and right beneath our feet. I suddenly realize that we have reached the boat.

Before I have the chance to see anything, someone is pushing me through a narrow opening. With arms outstretched before me, I grope around for a place to sit in this big black hole. The place is full of people, yet I am still being thrust forward. Finally, I am wedged in at the back of the room. I can't even breathe and I must be going blind. My left hand slips through a hole in the floor. The person next to me moves over to make room for me.

Since it is getting hot and stuffy here, I take off my sandals and remove my mother's scarf from around my neck. Someone whispers, "Don't make any noise, I'm opening the window" and I recognize Le Du's voice. A square, the size of a television screen, projects a corner of the sky and lets in a bit of fresh air. Under these gray reflections, I can make out the profile of an engine in the middle of the room. But I can't see Thanh anywhere. Is he on board? Oh, no! Not a catastrophe already!

The engine is noiseless...When are we going to leave? Every second on these shores can be deadly. Time is threatening. How much longer must I remain in this position? My legs are getting numb. I feel nauseous, but nothing comes up. For a minute I feel like jumping out of this cage and into the water, but that would be stupid. Feeling weak and helpless, I let my head drop to my knees like that of a slaughtered chicken. Only one thought keeps churning in my head: every moment seems to be an eternity!

The kind person who earlier made room for me says to me, "Stretch out your legs on me so that you can sleep. We'll take turns." The gentle voice of this girl or lady is like music to my ears. Discourteously, I accept her offer by slowly easing myself down on one side and extending my legs over her, with my head slightly bent at an angle. I say a short prayer and try to fall asleep. From across the room, a child's piercing cries suddenly shatter the stillness, tightening the noose of fear around everyone's throat. His cries are instantly muffled by the mother's hand. Finally, his suppressed sobs gradually subside. All we hear are rubbing noises as people jostle and move against one another, trying to settle down for the night in these cramped quarters. A nagging thought preoccupies me: tomorrow, as usual, the sun will rise in the East like a round ball of fire...But where will I be?

CHAPTER 11

OUT AT SEA

My body feels like an active volcano. Never in my life have I had such a rude awakening. When I opened my eyes, I saw Noah's world for the first time. The heat has already melted away yesterday's darkness and these weary bodies have absorbed it. Although the windows are closed, it is bright down here as my eyes scan the room in search of my brother. Relieved, I see him half-lying, half-sitting next to the engine, wide-eyed. The girl or woman who was so kind to me yesterday is still sleeping and bearing the weight of half my body. With great care I try to sit up without waking her, but I do not succeed. She eases herself up simultaneously, keeping her head bowed down; she must be saying her morning prayers. My neighbour looks at me. She must be in her twenties. Beautiful long hair frames her lovely smiling face. Each time I see a smile on a weary face, it reminds me of my mother. I wonder what she is doing right now.

Nearly everybody is awake by now. These people don't seem like strangers to me anymore, for the night has bound us in our common fate. But I still don't know who they are. There are at least thirty or forty of us crowded in here. This section of the boat is approximately three meters wide by four meters long and about one and a half meters high. But I have no idea how long the boat is. It is made of wood, inside and out. On both sides, there is a window big enough for someone to wriggle through like a snake. In the center stands a black, greasy engine with just enough room on either side for two people. In front of it, is a raised narrow platform beyond which is the entrance to the pilot house. So this means we are in the central part of the boat. It is not at all as I would imagined it would be. They told me it was going to be a big boat and I had thought of an ocean-going vessel made of steel. I also thought our destination was to be America or Europe, far away from this land of blood and tears. This little wooden boat could not be taking us across the ocean...

For some time now, there has been activity overhead. Gruff voices shout out orders. To our uninitiated ears, the bustling noises, typical at dawn in a busy fishing harbour, inspire a sense of dread. We feel like slaves destined for auction or like prisoners being carted off to sea to be ditched overboard, in the name of the law. We can hear several boats leave as their propellors swirl through the water.

A young man comes down to tell us that we must remain very quiet because it is our turn to leave. With some difficulty he tries to start the engine, which initially sputters and coughs to clear its throat before letting out a series of bellowing cries. The boat backs up, turns, and slowly moves forward.

People take advantage of the noisy engine to whisper to one another. The girl sitting next to me introduces herself: her name is Bach and she is also travelling with her younger brother. I explain to her that I am in the same situation. Although she is very nice, I am unable to keep up a conversation with her because I have a splitting headache and I feel like throwing up. Being only two feet away from the engine, I have to put up with its heat and gas fumes.

We are not moving very fast...perhaps the men are fishing? When will this torture end? Most of the people are nibbling on something or other to pass the time away. I don't dare eat because I know myself. My last experience has taught me to brave the waves on an empty stomach – I know the terror of motion sickness. Bach invites me to lie down as I did the night before and places a cool, wet handkerchief on my forehead. She takes care of me like a big sister.

Through the hatch leading to the pilot house, a pail of water and hankies constantly move up, down and around as in the dull stillness of a hospital. I don't need to look outside to know the sun is up because it is an inferno down here. The constant noise drowns out all peace of mind; exhausted bodies are almost mummified like cabbage rolls in this cooking pot. In hell, time cannot be measured for it is too long and too difficult to bear. Each swaying motion of the boat taunts me: why doesn't God hear my prayers? Why should I pray? And for whom? I have asked myself these questions before, but today they consume my mind. The other half is filled with fond memories which almost make me regret this trip. I see myself strolling hand in hand, with my father down the shady paths in the garden of Tao Dan. I remember those warm Sunday afternoons, the ice cream cones Grandmother bought us, and how we used to run barefooted in the pouring rain with our friends.

I look forward to nightfall, or rather, for the time to pass! When will we land? Something has got to change. We have been in this floating inferno long enough. This pagan day ends up putting the sun to shame, and darkness returns. The boat seems to have increased its speed. A rumour starts to spread like a cool salty sea breeze: we will soon be coming into port. I have no idea where that is. Women and children are being moved onto the platform. I almost have to crawl on all fours over bodies to reach it. Le Du explains that we won't feel the turbulence as much in this section of the boat. For the first time, I notice how few women and children there are in here: three small children aged four or five, and four girls (An-Ny, Bach, myself and another one). Everybody takes a pill against sea-sickness. Le Du hands me one also, but no sooner do I swallow it than everything comes up in my throat. I have no other choice but to gulp down this bitter, acidic substance...I have eaten leftovers from a plate left behind on the sidewalk by an American soldier, and jackfruit seeds which the merchants had thrown in the garbage can...Still, it is not easy to swallow this pill!

The engine seems to be slowing down...I can hear boats coming and going. Are we docking somewhere? Le Du's brother, who is a member of the crew, suddenly looks in through the forward window and whispers in a doom-filled voice, "It's the patrol boats; we'll have to open the windows; lie low to avoid their light beam!" Then he disappears and all the windows are opened. Here and there, people make the sign of the cross. I am starting to feel panicky. Intense beams of light pierce the darkness, shine through the window and sweep the walls. Like blades of grass bending in the wind, our bodies fold beneath its rays. I don't mind suffering but please don't let them take us back to shore.

How long does this last? Long enough to envision our lives coming to an end and rising again when the light and sounds of the threatening engines turn back into the night. The danger is over. Thank God! Our boat continues on its way, groping through thickening fog. A small night lamp bathes us in its yellow glow. Were it not for its constant flickering that makes me nauseous and these horrible ear-piercing noises, one could imagine we were spending a peaceful summer night on a countryside cruise.

But what is going on? I feel as though I am falling into a deep void as the boat pitches heavily and throws us against one another. Many are sick and moaning as they vomit in the bilge.

"Don't throw up in there, you'll block the pump," someone furiously shouts. So plastic bags are immediately distributed. After completely emptying out my stomach, I still feel the heaving throbs. Our vessel is prancing like a wild horse through a roaring, splashing sea. Since all the windows are shut, the heat and stench become almost unbearable. As for our ears, they are adjusting to the growling engine. Wrapped up in myself and immune to my surroundings, I try to control, or rather, bear each wave of nausea by reminding myself that each one brings me one step closer to my destination. My eyes are constantly focused on the opening of the plastic bag propped between my knees.

I recall the story of a saint who had been given a choice to make: either spend ten minutes in purgatory or thirty-six years nailed to a sick bed. I wondered why my mother told me this story? She never explained but today I think I know: whatever choice I make, I must accept, with total resignation, the pain it entails. "One must keep watch to know how long the night is." Time ceases to exist and the barrier between night and day disappears. Our evening and morning prayers merge into one to become the epic poem of a people in exile, glorifying its god for each victory over suffering and despair.

Boom!...Someone fell into the bilge. Startled, I think it must be my brother because he always tosses and turns in his sleep. But it isn't my brother and nobody is hurt. I feel limp as a rag and I don't even know who I am leaning against. After a while somebody moves, so now I can rest my back on something. I am hot and hungry. The boat's motion keeps me from sleeping.

Something is wrong with the pump. A mechanic comes down to see what the problem is, tries to repair it, then gives out an order, "You boys will have to keep bailing out the water that is choking the engine because the pump is not working." The boys work in two's, one inside, one outside, passing the pail back and forth through the open window at the rear of the cabin. I hate to think of what is in this liquid. Surprisingly, the boy who is lying face to the wall underneath the window doesn't even budge when the slimy water splashes on him from the shaky pail. It makes us realize that misery is now an integral part of our lives.

The sea is calmer now. Some say that the crashing waves last night were at least two meters high. Despite this improvement, I still feel sick. It is so warm and my throat is parched, but everyone is in the same position. Coping with the heat is not too difficult, but our thirsty bodies keep claiming their due. A jug of drinking water is being passed around. The water has a strange, undefinable taste, but at least its coolness satisfies our thirst. But when it reaches the pit of our empty stomachs, up it comes again, forcing us to use our plastic bags. After a while, thirst forces us back for more, then back to our bags...This is the way we undergo a collective "detoxification" treatment.

Is it still morning or mid-afternoon? What sea are we on? It is hard to believe we left just two days ago and that this is only the third day we have been shackled here. Will we ever land somewhere?

What's happening now? The boat is slowing down and stopping next to another vessel Where has it come from? It is impossible to make out what the discussion on deck is all about and everyone feels a sense of foreboding. Le Du's brother comes down to explain what's happening. We all listen to his every word.

"It's the coast guard" (which means we're still inside our country's territorial waters)..."They want us to hand over all our valuables and then they will let us go."

God have mercy and protect us! No shots are fired; that is reassuring. A hat is being passed around to collect rings, watches, earrings, silver chains, etc... One by one, these are sacrificed to buy our freedom. What should I do? I hesitate, remembering what my mother said about the ring, and decide to keep my cool. Nobody noticed I was wearing it because it was covered with thread. Surreptitiously, I slip it off my finger and into the cuff of my slacks. The hat is then sent up, but Le Du's brother returns saying, "It's not enough."

No reaction. One of the officers sticks his torso through the hatch. He is wearing civilian clothes, a soft cloth cap and dark glasses...as a disguise. He peers at us as though we are criminals headed for the gallows. All I feel towards this pirate is contempt and revolt but, like everyone else, I hide my repulsion. In this situation, we hold the knife blade whereas these officers hold the handle. People eye one another as if to say we have no more to give. One boy is still wearing three rings and everybody gives him a beseeching look. He feels embarrassed but doesn't seem to want to give them up.

"We need at least one more ring! Do you want to give them your ring now or when they take us back to shore?" one of the men angrily mutters to him.

After a moment's hesitation, the boy explains: "These three rings belong to five of us. I can't decide this alone. And besides, we've already given them two!"

Another young man, who is apparently the captain's son, decides to make a compromise with them. I don't understand what the deal is all about, but the boy with the rings finally gives in.

The officers finally leave and we are supposed to be grateful for their humanitarian gesture!...I hadn't been warned about such things, that is why I find it so tragic. But everybody else seems happy that it turned out so well! I don't dare ask what "normally" happens. As the boat starts moving again, my dizziness returns. The danger is over; now we can get back to our daily misery. Some say we will be in international waters within a few hours. Does that mean we will be arriving soon? Oh God, I can't wait! We are moving so slowly...But I must be patient. Fellow passengers return to their previous state of looking tired, sullen and withered. As I watch the boys resume their bailing efforts, I realize that the voyage is far from over.

To my left, Le Du and An-Ny are each holding a child in their arms. They are Le Du's niece and nephew whose parents are still in Vietnam. Quieted with pills, they are now fast asleep. Sitting on my right is the man who spoke to the boy with the rings a few minutes ago. A woman is resting her head on his shoulder; he offers me the other. Touched by the sincerity of his words, I let my head fall on his shoulder to rest my cramped neck. Leaning against my back is a young boy who looks quite ill. By now, my injured privacy has healed for we are all bound together like the planks of wood which form this vessel. Another boy sitting at my feet tries to comfort his young brother by hugging him tightly. Oh, if only our hearts and bodies could turn to stone while we await the day of our liberation... But we are all very much alive and sensitive to motion sickness and thirst. The drinking water, lukewarm and enriched with rust, is scarce so we are only allowed one gulp. Our sea adventure is a far cry from the romantic movies I have seen, where ocean liners waltz across the sea, and lovely sailing ships flap their sails in a joyous march.

Our wooden boat trudges along slowly in the scorching sun. The piping hot engine, the feverish bodies, the dry air...I want to close the lid on my coffin. I sit up in an effort to chase away these oppressive thoughts. I have a desperate urge to tear off the clothes that cling to my body and make me feel as though I am trapped in a giant cobweb. I can't stand this agonizing heat that is making my head throb. Noticing a narrow space between our cabin and the foreward hold, I decide to slip away from this nightmarish dungeon.

It is not easy to squeeze through. Someone has to help me by pushing my head – ouch, my ears! Like an overprotective brother, Le Du mutters some incomprehensible reproach. Now that I am in the other section, he can't scold me anymore. I feel like a mischievous child...It is very dark in here and I have to wait for my eyes to adjust to the dimness. It is also less crowded – only twenty people, and a little cooler too because we are away from the engine. The attractive young woman I met in that house the other night is here, lying next to her husband and two children.

There must be at least 15 centimeters of water in the bottom of the boat. And I realize it is the same slimy substance that was swooshing around the engine. Yet everybody is lying or sitting, soaked in this liquid. Noticing their immunity to the watery slime, I feel obliged to sit down in it too. When my behind comes in contact with this putrid pool I shudder, for I know very well what's in it: not just water, but also urine, vomit, and grease. Imitating the boat's motion, this liquid ebbs and flows, sometimes right up to my waist. The image of Jean Valjean in the sewers of Paris flashes through my mind and I feel great compassion for him.

Are we really all such wretched creatures? Are our bodies despicable because of circumstances, or are they rotten naturally? What makes us seek eternal perfection and purity? We have a body and a soul, but can a soul be imprisoned in such a body? And the God I pray to, where is He? Today, I am making the journey of my life. This road is my bridge of escape from a world of slavery and ignorance to the land of freedom, a border crossing between the depths of despair and the deep blue sky. At this mid-point, it is easier to believe in the existence of the "invisible".

These thoughts help me overcome my fear of the unknown but they do nothing to relieve my physical woes; now it is not the swaying boat that is making me nauseous but this slime I sit in! I am starting to regret having come here and I would love to change places. But there are only two possible exits from this cavernous hole; the slit from which I came down but through which I could never climb up again, and the hatch at the far end of the boat up to the deck where no one is allowed to go. There isn't a dry spot in the room, the water is everywhere.

Night has come, spreading its damp, mildewed hands over us like an evil ghost. Every wet part of my body feels itchy. I try to lean my head back so that I can sleep like the lady next to me, but because a wooden beam is in the way, I have to tilt it sideways. This hull beam is about 10 to 12 cm wide, so I figure I might as well try to sleep on it. One side of my body and my head are resting on it while the other leg soaks in the water to keep me balanced. But I don't know where to put my arms...The narrowness of my bed requires acrobatic concentration, but at least I am not completely soaked in water and I have something to keep my mind occupied.

Despite all the discomforts, I am consoled knowing that we are on our way. We will be arriving soon and I will work day and night. I will earn lots of money and I will come back to wipe away my mother's tears forever; I will plant smiles and sunshine throughout our house and we will relive our marvelous youth ten and twenty times over. How much money will all this cost? Can money buy all these things? Will I ever see my family again? Will we ever land somewhere? God, I know you always listen to the poor, and I am poor. Don't make me rich. Just give me the means to provide a little peace and serenity to the poor. Lord, is it too much to ask?

In this precarious position, my body aches terribly so I change sides. Now my head feels empty...time flows through it like the wind in a deserted house. In fact, what is the use of thinking and torturing my mind with unanswered questions? I am what I am. Still, I wonder...are we advancing in time like the pilgrims marching to the Holy Land, or is time coming towards us like an endlessly long train? One more question without an answer? One day, the questions will ripen and reveal their hidden essence.

The monotonous sound of the engine lulls the boat. Once in a while, the boys stop bailing out the bilge and life comes to a standstill, leaving the boat to sleepwalk in the night.

As the day begins, I feel restless and my eyes keep wandering up to that opening in the ceiling. The temptation to go up on deck takes hold of me, but I am afraid of everyone. The fear is stronger than the temptation, so I remain sitting on my beam. The man who is sitting at an angle from me looks a lot like my uncle who has been in a concentration camp (for five years now). Warmed by his sympathetic glance, I ask him when and where we will be landing. He goes on to explain that we have made a detour to avoid the Thai pirates; now we are heading for Singapore and the boat should dock by tomorrow. One more day; that is long, but I can wait. It is the first time anyone tells me where they are taking us.

A few of the men go up on deck and sit around the hatch with their feet dangling inside. I follow them to the exit and stick my head up through all these legs to catch a glimpse of the sky. When one of the men asks me what I want, I reply that I need to go to the bathroom (it is not true, but who cares!). Someone helps me up on the bridge. For the first time in four days, I can see the sky up above.

Every corner of the sea and sky looks the same. The only telltale sign that we are making headway is the swirling water streaming behind the stern. The sun reflections on the metal bars of the pilot house above are blinding me. A harsh voice orders me back inside but I pretend not to hear.

Here comes that nice lady who gave me a piece of her mandarin. As she steps out through the hatch, she says to me, "It's so warm down there."

"The sun is quite hot out here too," I add as she hands me a pail found on the bridge. With a mischievous smile, she implies that we can now enjoy the luxury of a bath. The same grumpy voice orders me in again. I guess they are afraid everybody will want to come out.

Squinting, the lady looks up to where the voice came from and says, "We'll go down in a minute after we've washed ourselves." What a brave lady! Her name is Lan. She must be about twenty or thirty years old (I am not very good at guessing people's ages). In turn, we pour buckets full of cool seawater over our filthy dehydrated bodies. For a precious minute, I forget all the problems and sorrows that have burdened my heart over the past fifteen years. Just as excited children play with a new toy, we splash our feet in the seawater and kick them wildly, faster and faster.

A man sitting nearby on the bridge startles us with his angry voice. "You want to keep your legs, don't you? Get away from the edge. The slightest movement of the boat could make you fall overboard...and the propeller would chop you up before the fish could feast on you."

I immediately pull back my legs as though I had just been bitten by a fish. Lan does likewise but her eyes mock my reaction and she bursts into laughter. My heart reaches out to this wonderful woman and I can't explain why I love her so much. With a bit more caution, we continue our bathing session by the side of the boat.

Suddenly there is a kind of a hush throughout the boat. Everybody is looking in the same direction. A mast of sorts is slowly emerging from beneath the sea. We can see a flag waving in the wind; it is a foreign ship. People start arguing about which country's flag it is, while the crew prepares to hoist a white cloth tied to the end of a pole. A distress signal is immediately sent out. Now we can almost make out its enormous profile. To what can I compare the size of this ship? When I look at its mid-section, I can't even see the extremities, and I have to practically break my neck to lean backward and see its flag . God, save us, please! Our fuel reserves are very low and we still haven't seen land. But, the big ship leaves, changing course. Did they see or hear us? And why didn't our captain go after it?

A tall, thin man steps out of the pilot house but doesn't come down. His face looks rugged and stern. His features seem to have been carefully carved by foreign sea winds. "Remain confident! We are in international waters where many foreign ships sail by," he explains. But he doesn't say why the big ship didn't respond to our signal. The kind gentleman who spoke to me down in the cabin this morning, tells me that it was an oil tanker and that this type of ship doesn't take on passengers. Lan and I continue to freshen up with the pail of saltwater, but with less enthusiasm. I try to compare my voyage to those I read about in books and I have admit that mine is not quite so wonderful.

Bach comes up on deck and joins us. Beads of perspiration stand out on her forehead, so I ask her if she wants to wash up a bit. Because she is afraid the saltwater might irritate her skin, she only washes her hands. Her camouflage shirt of green and brown speckles kindles the ashes of hidden memory; it is part of the Mao uniform, the symbol of an ideology.

The sun is so strong it even chases away the heavy clouds. Tiny salt crystals sparkle on my skin..."I see something", shouts a male voice. And we all recognize what he has seen. The boat stops and waits. Some of the people jump up and shout, waving their arms in the air. It is so exciting! Now we can see the main section of a flagless ship. Someone who is looking through binoculars, shouts to the crewmen, "There is a soviet insignia on the ship's hull." Now it is our boat's turn to take off at full speed.

We are no better off than the algae floating aimlessly on the surface of the sea. Who will pick it up and put it to good use? Weren't we supposed to land somewhere today? I keep asking the men around me if we will soon be arriving, but they always answer, "Maybe, maybe..."

Over the fire which was lit to send out our earlier distress signal, we try to distill some saltwater in a pot. But how can we stop the steam with an old piece of tin? Finally we must resign ourselves to watching the pot laugh at us as it sputters puffs of steam right under our noses. A young man comes to stand between Bach and me. His grave and mysterious countenance, his dark skin, his way of sitting, his precise gestures, remind me of a Tibetan monk. He scares me. He says that we should cook the rice in saltwater. I have often eaten rice with salt – perhaps this will be good too. The young man transforms the old piece of tin into a container for the rice and water. We all cluster around the fire to keep out of the wind. I haven't felt hungry for four days but now I am eager to taste this dish which will remind me of life in the civilized world. Blaah!...this sticky, crunchy rice tastes horrible! My mother always said rice had to be cooked in a covered pot. Nevertheless, I swallow the first mouthful because she also told me never to throw food away. Nobody else seems to like it either.

Hand in hand, the setting sun leads the day to another world. Mother must be getting ready to close up shop. She will be all alone to balance the books, alone like the moon. My eyes search the sea for a blue-haired mermaid who could visit my mother. But the sea has lowered her black veil. Off in the distance, a large dorsal fin is moving around gracefully like a figure skater: night has begun!

Several people retire below deck while others remain on the bridge. My brother has decided to join us. One of the men tells me to go in but I don't listen. I am always sick down there. So my brother and I stay out together, keeping very quiet. He must be exhausted from having to bail out the bilge these past few days. Like my mother, he has a strong constitution; he is never seasick. Although we are sitting side by side, we each inhabit a separate island in this vacuous ocean. We are two strangers linked by an invisible fraternal bond. And this bond is genuine and deep, for should there be danger, he would be the person for whom I would give my life. The wall of silence which separates us makes the sunset even more melancholy. I must try to break down this wall, if only for a minute.

To make conversation I ask, "At what speed is the boat moving?" He simply replies "fifteen kilometers per hour" and doesn't add another word. I have to be content to watch the darkening sky in silence. People stretch out on the bridge, listening to the moaning universe.

A man lying near the bow throws me an end of the heavy rope which he is holding in his hands. "Hold on to it, in case..." he says to me. I thank him and share it with my brother.

It is cold but I am not shivering. This coolness comes as a refreshing reward after a scorching day. I look at the sky and see the vault of heaven come down to crown our heads like the dome of a frescoed cathedral. When I look at such natural wonders, I want to cry. But these are not tears of sadness and sorrow. I cry because all things remind me that I exist!

It is already time to sleep. After feeling a few drops of rain on my cheek I get up, nudging my brother to tell him it is raining. Unmoved, he mumbles that he doesn't mind it. The gentleman who threw me the rope covers his head with a raincoat, sharing it with the person next to him. When I edge over to them asking for cover, they make room for me. Now I am lying near the open hatch. The man advises me to go down but I tell him I feel better up here. He doesn't insist. He is so kind but he smells awfully strange! It is a good thing the wind hasn't died down. The rain is really pouring down now and raindrops are playing a staccato fugue on our plastic keyboard.

We encounter several other ships moving in the night like giant red-eyed sea monsters. With a portable lamp, S.O.S. signals are sent out in Morse code. We are becoming less troubled by these unfullfilled expectations. The response to them is nothing but silence.

The rain howls, moans, laments, briefly stops, only to start up again even louder before being carried away by the wind. It reminds me of the souls of unfortunate soldiers wandering in search of their lifeless bodies.

Before dawn, I open and close my eyes as often as there are stars in the sky. The raincoat under which my good Samaritan sheltered me has been removed and, strangely enough, I am now lying at his feet. I sit up and listen to the dampness crawling beneath my clothes.

I await the coming of day like I used to do – sitting by the window, waiting for my father to come home. Punctually, my mother used to brush my hair every morning until I was five or six years old. "Now that you're a big girl, you can take care of yourself," my parents said when times got bad. So I became more and more independent. I grew up too fast and without enough time to be just a child. I was faced with countless questions...without solutions or answers. Now my mind and hands are bound by ignorance... This morning I feel resigned.

At last the sun is blazing down on us, wringing out our drenched bodies with its warm rays. Nature sings in exaltation, her face glows. But we are nothing but a horde of beggars who dare to set foot in a wealthy district. No, that is wrong. We are sinners walking toward John the Baptist.

We are told that we have been on the bridge long enough. Now we have to go in. Everybody goes down, so I can't very well stay here alone. I decide to go back into the engine room with my brother. I notice that Le Du is still sitting in the same spot and I don't know how he can stand it. Fatigue and exhaustion have probably made him listless. I too settle down in a corner and remain as silent as the grave. Thanh rolls his shirt and trousers into a ball, keeping only two pairs of shorts on. He hands them to me as I lie down and I use them for a pillow. There aren't as many people in here now because some of them went out. Thanh joins the other boys who are still bailing out the bilge and I just watch them, without comment. I can't help but feel wretched in this room: the engine keeps sweating and puffing out its poisonous fumes that make me dizzy. Even though the windows are open the air is stagnant and dank.

Nothing happens to rouse us. I can hear the universe winding itself up with a strand of time. One more day for the past, one less for the future. Time, they say, is like a bird flying by the window...but I see nothing moving through this boat's windows. The noonday sun forgets to blaze; at dusk the curtain of darkness falls without any applause to mark the end of its daily show.

CHAPTER 12

LIGHTS ON THE OCEAN

When will we arrive and where? For days, it seems we have drifted aimlessly and still the skyline remains empty. A flickering flame is bobbing over the distant waves. Perhaps this day will not end as quietly as it began! While the captain steers a course towards this glow, everyone is asking, "What is it?" Transfixed by the flicker on the horizon, I prop my chin on the window sill, oblivious to the nightfall.

We are not closing in on it as fast as I expected. Is it only a mirage? The flame is still out there like taunting bait floating beneath the sky. Suddenly, a whole city of lights looms up next to the flame but it can't be Paris! Many are so moved by this sight it is as though they are getting ready to say goodbye each with his own pack and destination. Our boat bravely forges ahead, no longer afraid of the night. As for me, I have one more reason to be anxious to set foot on land – the nausea. It has taken hold of me like a starving blood-sucker. But eagerness only makes time seem longer. I try hard not to delude myself too much about this city, but I can't help thinking about the long letter I will write to my family. The lights are getting brighter and brighter, and it is hard to tell whether it is the dawn or the city that has come to greet us.

We are already close. The tiny flame we saw earlier is now sitting majestically atop a huge chimney in the heart of this floating island; it looks like a giant candle! We are almost there. To my great surprise, there are no castles, no drawbridge...it is not even a city. It is a giant ship!

An endless fountain of light streams from the ship's festive lanterns. I am not disappointed that the light comes from a ship instead of a city. The ship is anchored, so it won't sail away. It does not bear the markings of a communist country so we will not sail away. We edge a bit closer to it but it is still submerged in sleep. The height of its ebony flanks makes me stagger. What if it fell over and came crashing down on us? We start coasting around the ship. All is still, not a sign of life. It takes us almost an hour to make a complete tour. We are like the ant in the fable, next to this elephant. We shout and scream but the echo of our voices is lost in the still of night. We finally stop at the spot where we first arrived so that the engine can catch its breath after days of back-breaking labour. The captain orders all the women and children up on the bridge, followed by the men. I can't wait to get out. What a relief! Everyone is squatting, hands joined in a prayerful manner, heads uplifted in the hope of seeing the face of a saviour appear up above.

The great ship gradually dims its powerful lights as the sun starts rising. Life on its bridge slowly awakens. Several silhouettes pass by but they don't see us. All together we shout and excitedly wave our arms. Startled by our cries, a blond man peers down from the railing. Dumbstruck for a minute, he disappears and returns with other crew members. The whole boat is trembling with excitement. No pen could possibly describe such happiness!

I immediately think of my family; now they can stop their plaintive prayer and burst into song because there are already a dozen men who have heard and seen us from above. Some are dressed in overalls, shirts or sweaters; others are bare-chested. A few of the men on our boat stand up and shout something to them in French or in English which I don't understand. They seem to be replying but we can't hear a word because of the ship's height. One of our crew members has an idea. He suggests we write a message on a piece of paper saying something like "Please save us!" The paper is then shown and waved to our benefactors. They understand immediately and a basket at the end of a rope is lowered down to us to collect our message of hope. The kind man who offered me his shoulder to lean on the other day kisses his rosary and places it in the basket. It is then hoisted up.

Ecstatic, we wait, while these men who speak a strange language try to decipher our note. After a good while, they send down a message of their own in the basket. A bearded man leans over the rigging holding the rosary in his hand. He crosses himself with it, indicating that he is also a Christian. He must be the ship's mechanic for his hands and clothing are soiled with black spots. We wave to him affectionately. The piece of paper in which our fate is wrapped is quickly unfolded. In his own words, the man who had written our message reads and translates the reply. "They're Norwegians and they sympathize with us, but they can't take us on board because they still have work to do here. They want to know what we need to continue our voyage, because the Indonesian Islands aren't far from here."

On hearing these last words, my eyes sweep the horizon, but all I see is sky and water. Their message only provides a faint glimmer of hope and the knowledge of an added stretch ahead. A second message is sent up, asking the Norwegians for water, fuel, food, clothing and especially the right course to follow. Once the basket brings them our second note, they go inside and return with everything we need, lowering it all down to us in several baskets, except for the water and fuel which arrive in forty litre containers. They even take off their shirts and sweaters and put them into the basket. This generous gesture chases away the beggar's complex from my heart. Each time a basket arrives, we hasten to see what is in it. All these gifts are donated to us by the ship's officers and crew. We eye the precious jewels avidly: apples, oranges, bread, sausages, clothing and even cigarettes.

In the last basket, we send up our words of thanks. After reading them, they gaily shout words which we don't understand, but it is obvious from the expressions on their faces that they are wishing us "bon voyage". They keep waving while talking and grinning, and we wave back energetically. All trace of weariness and fatigue seems to have disappeared from our dirty faces; our wild eyes and dry lips are now filled with merriment like snowball plants which are not afraid of the cold. These gallant Norwegians blow kisses full of tenderness to the women – a charming Western custom to which we do not know how to respond.

They go off to continue their work and we have to go back inside, missing the fresh air. The captain sets his course according to the Norwegians' instructions and we are on our way to a foreign country – Indonesia! I learned this word when I was in grade five but little did I think I would be repeating the lesson five years later! Why Indonesia? Weren't we supposed to go to America, or Europe? Where is this land of wealth and freedom? My stomach is acting up again. If only I knew we would soon be landing somewhere...anywhere, then I wouldn't complain. Everybody else seems to be more optimistic than I. The men are puffing on the same cigarette, passing it around. As they inhale that strange smoke and hold it in their lungs for so long, they seem to be feeding someone who is locked up within them. Then they exhale it, blowing white puffy rings in the air. Some people complain, but the cigarette keeps moving from mouth to mouth, disappearing into smoke.

People are wondering what to do with all the supplies we received. Our bodies haven't had nourishment for five days. A wind of discontent stirs the atmosphere. Already, abundance foretells of danger. We look like beggars waiting to snatch up the fallen crumbs from the master's table. An apple is divided into five, then ten sections, and we each get a piece. It reminds me of Sunday mass. But in the middle of this ocean, Sunday is no different from Monday, and here it makes no difference whether we share an apple or a piece of bread as long as the sense of "communion" remains.

We are each thinking private thoughts as we savor our juicy slice of apple. For me, this white fleshy pulp dressed in red and green silkskin has been a legendary object since I was five or six years old. One of my uncles, a very small man with a rounded smile who was a cook at an American army camp, would pass by our house on his bicycle some afternoons, and without stopping he would throw us a nice red or green apple and continue on his way. We would caress its soft skin gently for fear of bruising it. Delighted with this gift, we would sit and wait for Papa to come home. Big or small, he would always divide it into eight so we could each have a piece, just like we are doing today. My baby brother was born too late to know what an apple is and ...many other things.

"Oh, thank you," I mumble to the person handing me a piece of sausage the size of my thumb. It looks appetizing but I cannot bite into it; it is as hard as a rubber tire. Next to me, Bach is also wondering what to do with this meat. "It needs to be cooked," I say, and she seems to agree. We decide to keep our sausage for later when we have an opportunity to cook it. Wishful thinking – we don't know if we will ever land.

I can't wait to set foot on land again, but I am still worried. A sense of insecurity engulfs me and I feel like a naked ape in the middle of a dense jungle...I must get a hold of myself! I have nothing to fear. All I have to do is follow the others. Anyway, death is the worst thing that can happen to me and I am not afraid to die. So why worry?

Hazy smudges are starting to appear far out on the horizon. Tonight, our boat will be resting its bow at the foot of the prettiest Indonesian island, won't it? Tell me it is true, so that my stomach can relax and the afternoon can seem less palling. Bach and Thanh are already out on the rear deck. I would love to join them but I am afraid somebody might scold me. The boy who was blocking the exit while bailing out the bilge, has just stopped for a moment's rest. Now is my chance to sneak out.

The boys are having a whale of a time washing up in the water basin. Let's be quiet, for the sea is calm. Far out in the distance, the islands bathe in the late afternoon mist like immortal water lilies floating on a giant pond. When a thin, salt-and-pepper haired man steps down from the cabin behind the pilot house, I move over to let him pass. He greets me with a warm grin, "God willing, we will reach land tonight." No other stranger has ever approached me with such kindness!

Walking ahead of him is Bich – the girl who handed out bread to us the other day. She clutches him by the arm, calling him "Uncle Ban". Now he is spreading out a large, heavy blanket close to the edge of the boat to shield her while she washes up. How lucky she is to have an uncle to spoil her like that, even at her age. I am much younger, yet I am all alone to take care of myself. Why shouldn't I want what others have. When they return, I am touched by Bich's gaunt face marked by the ravages of sea-sickness. As Mr. Ban helps her climb up the stairs, I look away in order not to be reminded of my solitude.

Thanh and the other boys are sitting near the edge of the boat, arms wrapped around their folded legs. Like the sea, their countenance is dull and indifferent as they sit waiting for the bilge to fill up again. Suddenly a black dorsal fin slices through the ripples near the boat. Is it a shark? Before I have the chance to cry out, I notice that it is only a piece of timber. After a moment of stark terror, my courage returns and I ask my brother, "What kind of fish usually has such fins?

"Sharks", he says, "but they're not dangerous." I feel reassured.

He turns his head, looking out over the expanse and asks if I saw any flying fish. I simply shake my head and then inquire if he still has our cousin's address hidden in the folds of his trousers. This suddenly reminds him of the clothes he entrusted to me yesterday and which I completely forgot about. He stars blaming me for being careless. Sticking my head through the window to check if they are still there, I can't see them anywhere. "We'll find them," I scoff. But he gets mad because he is sure we will never see them again. Without raising his voice, he keeps on harassing me, saying that I am good for nothing and that I keep losing everything. Now that is an insult! After all, aren't I his big sister? I am beside myself with rage and it is only out of respect for the crowd that surrounds us that I manage to reply evenly "If we don't find your clothes, somehow I'll find a way to get you other ones; do you understand?"

Despite my self-control, I know my words have the effect of a sledge-hammer. Abruptly, Thanh bolts up to sit farther away in order not to hear me. Now he is really adding fuel to the fire. I look around for a harmless object with which I can vent my anger. "There is no use getting mad at the fish when you have cut the board in half," my mother would say when I got angry. I am surprised that I recall these words today before smashing or ripping up something. I stay away from my brother so I won't have to see him pouting or so I won't have to talk to him.

Clouds, like smudged charcoal, turn the afternoon to dusk. Lost in contemplation, Bach is sitting outside the cabin where Bich came out of earlier. She motions me over to join her. A young boy is lying down next to her, eyes closed and forehead marked with fatigue. I can guess it is her brother even before she tells me. "His name is Luc", she says. Pointing down to the bare-shouldered Thanh, I also introduce my brother. Happy to get acquainted, we smile at one another. Her simple, unaffected ways quickly win my affection. I hate social courtesies, but Mother taught us to be polite and I love showering flowers of kindness. When Bach gently feels her brother's forehead, every feature in her pretty face twitches with anxiety. "Luc is sick," she explains with a pained look in her eyes. I suddenly feel a mixture of compassion and shame. All four of us are in the same situation, but at least between these two, there is love and affection whereas between my brother and I...there is only squabbling.

We get along splendidly with our new friends. Luc is awake now but too weak to sit up. We talk about everything close to our hearts: our families, our streets, our schools... It is comforting to know that I have a new family now. There is a proverb that says, "A tree alone does not a hill make, but three trees together form a mountain." Together, we four will manage better. One of Bach and Luc's younger sisters, who remained in Vietnam, has the same name and age as I. That is why they consider me like a sister. It is wonderful to make oneself small and inconspicuous with those you love. I regret now having been so angry at my brother. A jug of drinking water is being passed around. This water the Norwegians gave us is so distilled it doesn't taste like water anymore. Bach gives Luc a drink while I lean my back against the cold aluminum siding.

CHAPTER 13

LAND

The nocturnal stillness is shattered by a voice commanding everyone to go inside. We are going to reach land soon. Not wanting to prolong this voyage any further, I promptly go down and I obediently re-enter the engine room – a city damned by the God of fire, if not a crematorium! Tangled bodies wriggle and push to settle in. I manage to cross over to the far end where Thinh (Tuê's brother) saves a spot for me next to him close to the window. He already has his small knapsack on his back, a greeting on his lips and a head full of projects. In other words, he is ready to disembark. His friendly smile soothes my inner turmoil. It is amazing how hope can create such bonds of affection between us and transform this volcanic milieu into a haven of newfound camaraderie.

The room is terribly overcrowded now. Bach, Luc and Thanh have managed to find a place to sit. Bach remains alert at all times; her doggedness reminds me of my mother. Luc is leaning against the wall, and not far from him, Thanh is snoozing like a kitten. All the other faces look familiar because of this part of our lives that we have shared. I avoid looking at Le Du because I am still intimidated by his stern face.

Fresh air currents are rare in here and my stomach is heaving. As I try to ease myself up to the open window to catch a breath of fresh air, Thinh gently advises me to get some sleep before the boat reaches land. But he remains wide-eyed and ever ready. Sleep can wait for me too because I don't want to miss the landing. We can already see the beacon – this watchful eye of the islands surveying the traffic at sea.

The beacon slashes the veil of night, but darkness immediately blocks the path before us until the beam returns. Our little boat recites the sailor's creed for renewed strength and heads for the lighthouse. Suddenly the bow is flooded with light, making every head perk up. We are arriving, but are we going to land in the dark? Why doesn't the captain go closer to the lighthouse? We are much too far from shore to get off and we can barely make out the shape of the islands. Instead, we coast along the islands, leaving the beacon behind. I frown with impatience and incomprehension; at the same time, I feel sick to my stomach.

Next to me, Thinh's eyes are scanning the deep night. When the straps of his knapsack slip down from his shoulders, he doesn't bother adjusting them. Everybody is asking questions about our destination. Ignorant of the captain's plan, we remain calm and trusting. The captain must have his reasons. Maybe he is not heading for shore because of the reef? We don't even know if these islands are inhabited by humans or wild animals. There is nothing to indicate that this is Indonesia, or that we are welcome here. All we can do is wait for the night to swallow the stars and for the sun to announce the dawning of a new day. But why doesn't the captain anchor and wait? Is he afraid we might find ourselves on the back of a whale? I know this sounds crazy, but I can't see any other reason why he keeps going on. I am always talking about the captain, but I have never even seen him. As for the crew, I only know Le Du's two brothers. I suppose it is not necessary to know someone, to trust him. I want to believe in someone and understand him at the same time! Let's not be impatient! We have to take things as they come. At last, dear God, we are arriving. I am choked up with emotion, but...is it one of joy or of fear? Our Father who art in heaven, grant us peace, please!

Coming out of nowhere, three Indonesians paddle towards us in their pirogues. They look like the Philippinos I met during the war. Like Vietnamese peasants, they are wearing cotton scarves on their heads. They... I can't see them anymore because the boat is stopping. An air of expectancy permeates the cabin. Emotions of joy are mixed with the fear of what lies ahead. Not knowing what's going on outside, I am very nervous.

The engine sparks to life again but we move very slowly this time, following the dugout canoes. People start gathering their belongings. I look for my sandals, my scarf and my brother's clothes, but they have all disappeared without a trace. When I enquire about them to Le Du, he says they threw everything that was useless overboard. These words produce a jabbing pain in my heart and I have to bite my lips in order not to cry. When I remind him that my mother gave him my medication, he tells me that he doesn't have it anymore. I have had no food or medication for five days. I have conquered the typhoid fever and I am not afraid of illness anymore. But I must find some clothing for my brother. The young man nearby is stuffing his clothes in a bag, so I ask him if he has any to spare for my brother. He says he will have a look. No luck! I don't feel like haggling so I don't insist. Downhearted and faltering, I edge over to the window again. Must I beg everyone carrying a bag to share a bit of clothing with me?

Our boat is still following the pirogues. Our petty lives are somehow like this boat. One morning we wake up and realize that we exist, so we abandon everything to blindly follow an unknown course to an uncharted destination. There are as many inner recesses in this bay as there are alleyways in our neighbourhood.

We are really going ashore. At the entrance to the island, there are many wooden boats like ours, but bigger, jostling one another like impatient hordes queuing in front of a state-run shop. Along the shore, a humble dock dips its feet in the water like an old fisherman enjoying a pleasant day.

Before I know it, we are mooring. An officer in military garb walks over to our boat and stands at the end of the dock. His dignified stance indicates that he is the military commander on the island. Heading towards him is the man who wrote our message to the Norwegians. The officer's expression is as hard and cold as the revolver strapped to his waist. I dread to think of what will happen. When our spokesman returns, everyone is out on the bridge. What do we do now? "Just do like everybody else and everything will be fine," I tell myself. I must try to keep calm...like I used to when I had to stand in line for vaccinations at school. I suppose this representative will register our names and dates of birth. "Now, Doan, keep your eyes open and see what you must do," I tell myself.

Some say we should change our ages...in case of conscription; it is safer to claim to be younger. Who knows – what if there is a war? We mustn't be eighteen before we are able to work. Now let's figure all this out. We need time to get to America or Europe, time to learn the language, time to master a trade...And maybe that won't even be necessary because I am willing to do anything. If I say I am four years younger, it might be easier to find a foster home for my brother and myself. The younger you are, the less people try to harm you. Four years...even Mother made herself younger by two years when she went into exile and it didn't show at all. Also they say that westerners are bigger in stature than we are. For once I think my idea makes sense. Motioning to Thanh to come closer, I tell him about my plan. He approves it, and now it is our turn to speak up.

"Doan, September 15, 1968 and Thanh, November 13, 1969," I softly reply to my interrogator, watching for his reaction. Nothing! He didn't even look up at us. Once this formality is over, we crawl on hands and knees to keep our balance as we try to reach the stern to disembark. Those already out help us climb onto the dock. Even the Indonesian chief comes over to greet us with a friendly smile. I open my mouth to utter a response, but nothing comes to mind.

Utterly embarrassed, I lower my head and walk on. I glance back to check the sincerity of his smile; he is bedecked with medals, but the prettiest one is on his lips.

Le Du is already out on the dock with An-Ny, his niece and nephew, all of whom are sitting on top of their baggage. "We must go over and see them," I whisper to my brother. "After all, they are in charge of us during this trip."

The dock is waltzing beneath my feet! Am I drunk or something? With concentrated effort, I manage to walk half-way down the dock to join Le Du's group. Looking very tired, he inquires how we are. His brother Cuong arrives with a box of clothes. "Why, that's the clothing we received from the Norwegian ship," I exclaim and I ask him if I could have one piece. Without saying a word, Cuong hands me a pink sweater. In a jumble of words, I thank him profusely. My eyes must be sparkling like those of a cat in front of a plateful of fish.

When I show my brother the sweater, he pointedly tells me to keep it. I don't know what to say to him without start-ing another fight. Since he doesn't seem angry, I decide to keep the sweater. It still smells of the donor's perspiration. From a short distance away, the two brothers, Tuê and Thinh, wave us over, greet us warmly and enquire how we are. "Thank God the worst is over. Now that we are in this strange land, we must help one another to survive. If you ever need anything, don't hesitate to ask for our help", says Tuê with affection. "Will you be staying with Le Du?" he asks with concern.

When I reply that I don't know where we will be stay-ing, Tuê promises to take care of the matter. My face is beam-ing with gratitude, but his solicitous attention makes me feel sorry for myself and I have to fight back the tears. Bach and Luc are coming, so we leave Tuê and Thinh to go over and join our friends. Together we sit down and wait to be told what to do next. When I ask Bach to explain the meaning of my dizziness, she tells me it is normal to feel this way after five days on a boat and that it will soon pass. I show her the sweater I got; Bach thinks it is very nice. Realizing suddenly that Thanh doesn't know them very well, I proceed with a brief introduction. After exchanging a few words, fatigue plunges each one of us into our own separate thoughts.

Completely empty by now, our boat joins the other decrepit vessels rotting alongside the dock. I presume they have all been through a similar experience. Other refugees must have arrived in this port of call! I wonder what has become of them? But these boats gravely guard their secrets. And ours still doesn't know that its engine will be removed and that time will torture it to death. But a good sailor is not afraid to die. Even though I never knew a minute of happiness on that boat, I will never forget it. Its motor is roaring with laughter one last time before being torn away from its housing. I don't begrudge it for making me so sick, because it was brave and never gave up on us! In a faltering voice, it mutters a final farewell... When its heart stops beating, the helmsman comes out. Henceforth, this deserted vessel will be the tomb in which the enslavement of our goals and ignorance is buried. Many a monsoon will weep on this sorrowful citadel and enshroud it with dead leaves...

A boy dives into the sea's giant basin for a refreshing bath and climbs back on board one of the abandoned boats to dry himself off. The rippling waters have quieted and through a crack in the dock, I can see right down to the bottom. All sorts of fishes are swimming around down there. No, I would rather remain filthy than risk being torn to shreds by those sharp-toothed monsters.

CHAPTER 14

KALAMOU

The Indonesian chief is still carrying on a conversation with those of us who speak English. I notice that the men who came to meet us in their pirogues and the soldiers have all left. We are being ordered to proceed inland. Bach takes me with her. Promising to join us later, Luc goes off to take care of something, and Thanh accompanies him.

As we follow the others to go and wash up, the earth keeps swaying beneath my feet; it is as tiring as walking on a tightrope. Finally we reach a well. There is not a single house in the vicinity, yet several Indonesian women are here filling up their water jugs. Men and women bathe together around the well. Of course, we wash with our clothes on. A bar of soap slips from hand to hand. Gallantly, the men keep handing loaded pails of water to the women. Peels of laughter and joyful banter accompany this refreshing ritual. Bach is being teased by a tall young man to whom she replies with an broad grin, "It's only because you're my cousin that I put up with your jokes." He laughs and then leaves her alone. Bach turns to me and says, "That's Phu. His father, Mr. Ban, is my uncle."

Stunned, I reply, "So Bich is related to you?"

"Yes, she's my cousin. Her father, Mr. Nghi, is the owner of the boat," Bach explains while she continues to wash up.

This news saddens me. So Bach and Luc aren't alone like I had thought. They have a family with them. "A drop of blood is worth more than a crystal clear lake." Because Thanh and I are strangers, we do not have the right to impose on this family. In order to hide the tears trickling from the corner of my eye, I immediately empty a pail of water over my head.

Luc and Thanh are coming back. While Bach is talking to her brother, I ask Thanh to lend me one of his pairs of shorts. I am surprised to see him with his shirt in hand. "If I hadn't kept it , you would have lost it for good too," he retorts, heading for the well with Luc. I am glad my brother is not alone. Boys get along better together. We continue showering but I avoid getting too close to the well because I still feel very dizzy.

After this welcome cleansing, I hide behind the trees to change. I look thinner and whiter than before my bath. Over my wet underclothes, I slip on my brother's shorts and the Norwegian sweater – it almost reaches down to my knees! But I have no complaints – Bach isn't so lucky. She has to keep all her wet clothes on. Together we go for a walk while my clothes are hung out to dry in a tree. Barefoot, we carefully step over the rocks and dried branches. The others are scattered in small groups in the forest composed mainly of banana and coconut trees. Beyond the bushes, we find a toilet. Although it is rather primitive, it reminds me of the civilized world. In what way do our present living conditions differ from those of wild animals? Perhaps ours are simply more difficult to accept. Wise people say that in order to be happy, "One must forget the past, try to cope with today and trust in the future." But how can I? I am plagued with the past, ignorant of the present and worried about the future. On what soil must I lay my bricks of patience and pour the concrete of willpower to build a happy home?

Just as we are getting ready to leave, a dozen young Indonesians march by, one after the other, each carrying a long knife and staring at us. Their blank, indifferent faces seem to be chasing us away with contempt. We all remain paralyzed with fear. Only when they finally disappear into the forest do I snap out of this nightmare and start walking with the others. I hear people from our boat chatting together on the hill up ahead.

Before reaching them I notice a wooden house nestled beneath broad shady branches. Its mistress is a friendly-looking old lady. Bach addresses her with a respectful greeting which the old lady guardedly acknowledges. Leaving us standing in the yard, the lady goes back into the house where she seems to be living alone. I think to myself with dread that she might cast an evil spell upon us. But the old lady returns carrying two cups of tea and no curse. I am still thinking it would be ridiculous to die for a cup of tea. However, I decide to drink up like Bach is, under the watchful eyes of this grandmother. She is trying to tell us something, using sign language and pointing to the coconut trees. I don't know whether she is trying to tell us to eat these coconuts or that we are not allowed to pick them. Anyway, we mustn't take advantage of her kindness. On one hand, I am deeply grateful as we hand back the cups. On the other hand, I wish Bach would hurry up and leave this lady. My smile is a bit forced but the old lady's expression is not ominous or condescending; on the contrary, she is wearing a constant grin. Yet those young people we just saw were also Indonesians!

We leave her to join up with the others on the hill. My dizziness is tiring me out. I must be careful not to step on the ant hills because these vicious insects can burn you like fire. Beneath the trees, like clusters of mushrooms, people squat in groups of three or four. Neatly washed and combed, Luc and Thanh greet us with a smile while Bach tells them about our encounter. Everyone looks happy. I don't understand; is the danger really over? In a kindly mocking tone of voice, the man who gave his rosary to the Norwegians says to me, "You have a lovely sweater, young lady!"

Embarrassed and offended, I turn my back on him, pretending I don't hear. "Take it easy on her, Hao!" retorts another man.

"Don't you pay any attention to their stupid remarks," Bach whispers to me.

The boys have borrowed a large knife from someone and they are using it to crack coconuts open. I don't know if they asked permission to cut them down. "Do you want some?" asks Luc, winking mischievously. Before we can reply, he is already climbing up the tree like a monkey. Three coconuts come thumping to the ground as Luc slithers down as fast as he went up. The juice from this fruit is flavorful and sweet.

A boy comes over to talk to Bach and Luc. He is the boat-owner's son and is also their cousin and he has the same name as my brother. They talk about the matter of the "rings" and "pirates" on the boat the other day. Since I don't understand anything about this, I look away, tongue-tied with fear and bashfulness. Moving over to sit on a tree trunk, I silently listen to the conversation.

It seems there were sixty-five of us who made this voyage. The name of this mysterious island feigning sleep beneath our feet is Kalamou. It is part of an Indonesian archipelago. These are some of the things which caught my ear during the conversation.

Birds returning to their nests are scolding their greedy fledglings. The lazy midday sun peeks through the branches while the wind plays heads or tails with the leaves. It is all so lovely, so peaceful, but it is not mine!

At the foot of the hill, we start preparing our evening meal. The men are cooking rice on an open fire and I note that none of the Indonesians are with us. I feel embarrassed because after all, this isn't our land. Someone hands us two pink fishes to clean with a blunt knife. Luckily Bach is more adept than I at this. One of the men arrives, proudly displaying a large blue fish which the local fishermen probably gave him. I wonder if it isn't too blue to be edible! Seasoned with the cooks' humour and a bit of sand, the rice is a welcome feast for our shrivelled stomachs. We eat it with our clean hands. But I don't get to taste the fish – we mustn't have prayed hard enough to obtain another miracle of the fishes...

After the meal, Bach, Luc, my brother and I sit together and talk. Not far from where we just ate is an uninhabited house; all the doors and windows are shuttered. Some of the crew members walk up to its verandah, leaving bags of dried food which had been prepared for the voyage. I can't understand why we never got to eat any of it. Clenching her teeth, Bach gives them an awry look and says, "If I had some of that flour, I could make you a good meal tomorrow."

I suggest that we go and get some. After all, it belongs to us. Since children are considered more innocent, we decide to send Thanh to accomplish this mission. "Go and get the bag of flour on the verandah, Thanh. Don't be afraid. You know that Mother had prepared several four kilo bags of it for us."

Just as he is about to grab the bag, someone walks up and demands to know what he is doing. Almost in a stutter, he replies that Bach wants a bit of flour. "Who is this brave young lady named Bach?" asks the man in an authoritative and scornful voice. Thanh nods his head in our direction and the man looks over at us without saying a word. Then he addresses a few threatening words to my brother before letting him leave – with the bag in hand. When Thanh returns, we all laugh at what happened.

The Indonesians are back and rounding us up...Maybe they want to put us up for the night. The chief makes a sign for Bach and me to follow him. Not knowing what is happening, we give each other a worried look. Thanh and Luc don't want to leave us alone, so they come along as we follow the chief to the village, not knowing where the others will be going. We are being led down a narrow path paved with white pebbles.

The sun has fled, abandoning us to our nighttime fate. Dogs sadly yelp at the graying scenery. There are so many people in this village, it is as though we are walking through an open beehive. As the leader cuts a path through the crowd, both sides of this gentle slope are lined with children, and the adults stare at us from their verandahs. I try to smile at the children but I keep remembering the faces of the knife-toting youths I saw earlier. They don't like me, I can tell. They are hissing and scoffing at us as the boys touch me brutally. My eyes cry out for pity but they only laugh at me. With downcast eyes focusing on Bach's heels, I continue my Way of the Cross. But why aren't they touching Bach? When I consider what I must look like, I think that perhaps they want to see if I am a boy or a girl. Because of my close-cropped hair and odd clothes, they wouldn't be able to tell my sex. I hope it is not because they hate foreigners!

The chief leads us into a big house which must belong to a very important man in the village. He leaves us alone in the living room and goes over to talk with members of the family in the next room. I feel more relaxed that we are away from the excited horde outside. Then he walks out of the house, abandoning us like sacrificial lambs in these un-familiar surroundings...But we are not alone for long! An Indonesian man walks in – he seems to be the master of the house – and turns on the radio without so much as glancing at us. Then he starts removing his sarong. My heart sudden-ly stops beating; there is panic in the air. Totally ignoring our presence, he puts his trousers back on and goes out with the radio.

When the other family members come in to talk to us, I don't have the chance to speak to Bach. Three women and several children greet us kindly – unlike the horde outside a while ago. Our conversation is limited to gestures, inter-spersed with a few words of English. Once in a while, there are interruptions when everyone gets up to chase after a cen-tipede or some other insect. Bach entertains the children with her singing. The boys, Luc and Thanh don't talk much. All I do is watch out for those nasty creatures. I dread cen-tipedes because I was bitten by them once and had to go to a witch doctor for a cure. Bach is still playing with the children but her eyes often dart to the door in the hope that someone else will come to join us. At last, Bach's cousin Hô arrives.

One of the women asks Bach whether I am a boy or a girl – so I was right a while ago, and that was why the boys were touching me. She immediately goes into another room and after a few minutes she returns with a pair of slacks in her hands. She throws them over to me, indicating that I should put them on. My few words of thanks in English are greeted with a smile. Next to selfishness, language is the greatest barrier between nations.

When bedtime comes, the family retires. All five of us stretch out to sleep on the concrete floor of the living room. When the light is turned off, each one whispers a silent prayer. I ask the Lord to protect us tonight because I am afraid we are in imminent danger. When I close my eyes, all I can see are centipedes, spiders, lizards crawling everywhere... Frightened, I open my eyes, and up on the ceiling I see all the Indonesian faces I have encountered today.

Just as I finally begin to sleep, the chief enters and orders us to follow him. His bronze face reveals nothing of what is happening. Obediently, we follow him back to the sea. There is nobody outside...it is all so confusing. Sharp rocks are bruising my feet. When we finally reach the shore, I notice that the people from our group are being loaded onto two boats. An Indonesian pushes me and two or three others into another boat. It is so crowded that the slightest movement could easily make it tip over. Slowly easing my way through this human jungle, I end up near the edge and almost fall overboard. Every jostle and push brings me closer to the edge and I cling to the rail. I can't hang on much longer. In military silence, the Indonesians finally manage to balance the load in each boat and everybody is sitting quietly. Thanh is with me but Bach and Luc are in the other boat. Are we doomed to be separated forever? When the engines start roaring, I shudder at the thought that the village might rise up and throw a hex on us.

We are back at sea but no longer masters of our destiny. When I was a little girl, an old lady had predicted that I would die at sea. Although the ocean was far away from home, this prediction always scared me. Today I am part of a wandering tribe, rocking and floating from one shore to another. I am afraid of everything.

We have just stopped in the middle of a bay. The engine noises are gobbled up by the deep blue waters. The Indonesians bustle about arranging things of which I know nothing, then the boat which accompanied us returns to shore. As it heads back, we remain perfectly still. Why are they abandoning us here? Somebody whispers that an Indonesian remains in the cabin. Everyone is quiet now as we try to sleep and pass the time. A little boy is already sleeping in his brother's arms next to me. The older boy moves over so I have a place to lean my back. Like a cat sprawling on a fence, I manage to stretch out on the narrow toe-rail. The phantom of sleep gently calls and the night is still, but for the lulling sounds of insects. Once in a while, the darkness heaves a morbid sigh. The islands breathe and dream along with us.

I am freezing cold and I think I have fallen overboard. Sitting up, stark terror charging through me, I realize I am still on board and dry. Now where is my sweater? A gentle breeze flutters over the boat wet with dew. Side by side, like a pair of shoes lying at the foot of a giant's bed, our two boats are sleeping soundly. Having retrieved my sweater, I lie down again, cover my bare arms with it and quickly fall asleep.

Did the rooster crow? I don't know, but dawn has arrived. The others awaken with a stupefied, sleepy look on their faces. I am glad to find that I am still on board and that nothing happened to disturb the night. When I finish saying my morning prayer, the sun is already up. The peaceful islands surrounding us are flanked with wooden and concrete houses. Suddenly a loud and startling cry shatters the stillness. I soon realize that it is a prayer cried out by one muezzin in a minaret rising up to heaven like a kite snapped up by the wind.

It is much warmer now than last night, so I fold up my sweater and slacks. These are precious to me, even though they are as stiff as rice cakes and covered with mildew spots.

Here comes the boat that accompanied us last night. Again, we gather our belongings and prepare to board it. This Indonesian boat is a little bigger than the fishing boat we arrived in. When all sixty-five of us have boarded the vessel, we leave. Bach and Luc are with us again, wondering why we ended up in different boats. But that is not important now because we are so happy to be together again.

I have no idea where they are taking us. My face is contorted from the effects of the sun and my wretched stomach. I am too exhausted to move, but my eyes are wandering in search of our next port of call. There are so many islands out there, forming a chain around the earth's neck.

CHAPTER 15

AIRRAYA

Although the boat is moving fast, the time seems to stand still. At last we reach our next destination – a dream island. We step out onto a wooden dock which is branding my feet like red-hot irons! Those who still have shoes quickly take them out of their bags whereas the barefooted ones have to hop from one foot to the other while waiting for the welcoming party. For a short while, a cloud shields us from the sun. Now I can see a bit better. The beach is empty but people are waiting for us at the end of the dock. They are Vietnamese! But...we are not in Vietnam, I hope? A man is standing on a platform holding a microphone in his hand. "Welcome to the Airraya refugee camp..." Bored from standing still, the cloud moves away, letting the sun blaze down on our heads. The voice over the microphone invites us to enter the island after undergoing certain formalities. We march down the long, ferry dock. I am frightened by the crowd up ahead, even though I know they are also Vietnamese refugees. As we set foot on the soft, burning sand, I glance around to make sure Bach, Luc and Thanh are close by me.

As the inhabitants of the island jostle and push to get a glimpse of us, their smiles are a welcome sight. But the jostling stops and disappointment appears on several faces; they don't see any of their relatives in our group. Questions spring from all directions: "What city are you from?" "How many are you?" "Any pirates?" etc... I let the others answer because I feel too tired to speak. Every reply brings back memories of those interminably long past six days. How many more days of waiting will there be? The camp director then leads us to a waiting room. It looks like a garage full of wooden benches. As we enter, each one is obliged to take two yellow pills with a glass of warm water. From the bitter taste, I can tell it is quinine – to protect us against malaria. Then we go and sit down to rest on the benches. People of all ages come over to talk to us., The sun continues to bother me! It is even chasing after us beneath this roof. Our sweaty, sand-covered bodies belie last night's bath. At the equator, spring weather is as fierce as summer weather!

One of the young men seems to be paying a lot of attention to the four of us. After introducing himself, he asks, "Are you hungry?" This is the first time in a week anyone has asked us that question. The answer is quite evident but Bach gives him an affirmative reply in a very nicely worded way. "I'll get you something to eat, then we can talk!..." says our good Samaritan. Several minutes later, he returns with two pieces of bread and a can of fish. I am not hungry but my empty stomach seems to be growling "mercy" at the sight of bread. Having no ustensils, we simply dip the bread in the sauce and eat the fish with our fingers. The young man's name is Hung. He is a mechanic and hopes to settle in the United States.

"How long must we wait here?" we ask. According to Hung, it depends on how long we have to stay on each island before meeting with representatives from the free countries who will assess our qualifications for resettlement in one of these countries. Apparently those who already have relatives over there, are the first to go. Luckily Bach and Luc have a sister in West Germany and we, a cousin in the United States.

The camp director attracts everyone's attention by announcing the program for the day: registration, vaccinations, medical check-ups and distribution of basic supplies. He also points out that we will only be here a few days since we chose to flee the country rather than buy our way out. The next island will be Galang. And he concludes his speech with kind wishes and words of encouragement to all.

As we prepare to line up with the others for registration, Hung leaves. promising to come back and see us tonight. When we walk up to the registration clerk, we give him our names and ages (i.e. 4 years younger) and wait for a reaction. But none comes. Absolutely none! Then we give him our cousin's address and he hands us a card for our physical. Bach and I then line up with the women who are waiting to be vaccinated. After looking at our cards, the two nurses give each other a funny look. Pointing to Bach, one says to the other, "eighteen" and then "twelve", as she points to me. I turn pale and my legs start to shake. Is it so evident that I lied about my age? Dear God, what can I do? It is too late to cry; what is said is said and the spoken word is irretrievable. I must try to forget the whole thing and time will take care of everything. Lying is horrible!

In front of the Health Center, we have to squat on the ground because the place is full of people. I avoid talking to Bach about what's worrying me. This age problem is weighing me down. I guess it is true that dying is much easier than living...I must be coming down with a cold because I am sneezing; no, it is blood! Bach runs to get me some toilet paper. She also lets me go in ahead of her for my medical. It is not a very complicated examination; Their questions are about my previous illnesses not my age.

Luc and Thanh have gone to get some food and two blankets. Now we are being led to the reception hall. It is simply a large hall with a roof on top and several small adjoining rooms. I don't know how Bach and Luc managed it, but we are settling in with Mr. Nghi and his three children in one of these rooms. Most of the others remain in the big hall. There are also a few small houses in the vicinity. Except for the information center and health center which are made of tin, all the other buildings are built out of logs, green plastic and crowned with thatched roofs. It is a quaint little village!

After doing the dishes, we go and bathe in the nearby stream while the men do the same, but further upstream. Bach and I choose a spot where there are plenty of bushes. Trying to change clothing is a real puzzle – we want to keep something dry to put on, yet we don't want to bathe in the nude.

Suppertime comes, marking the frontier between afternoon and evening. When we enter the hall to pick up some canned food and rice, Mr. Nghi is busy whittling something out of wood. "You'll have chopsticks to eat your supper with tonight," he says as we head out to prepare the meal in the communal kitchen – a square sandy area outside.

Quite a few people are eating their dinner around the cooking pots set on the ground, but my brother and I feel like strangers among them. Even though I am quite hungry, shyness takes the edge off my appetite. It was very kind of Bach and Luc to consider us as family, but still we mustn't impose upon these good people. On the other hand, if it weren't for Mr. Nghi, we wouldn't even have any dishes to cook and eat our meals in. I feel so lost, so very much alone.

Bach suggests we go for a walk after clearing away the dishes and putting things back in place. Night has fallen and in the balmy breeze, floats an ocean scent. Just as Bach and I are about to leave for our walk, I hear Le Du calling me. Alone, I walk over to greet him and smile at An-Ny, who is by his side. In a serious tone (unlike that of a bossy big brother but of one who is concerned), he says, "I promised your mother that I would take you under my wing and I don't want you to wander around on your own. You can come and stay with us. An-Ny can help, because among women..." But she cuts him off, exclaiming, "Don't you think I have enough taking care of the two children?"

To spare Le Du any further embarrassment, I quickly explain that we appreciate their concern, but that we are not alone. Bach and Luc consider us as their brother and sister. "That's good!" he sighs with relief. "I'll send a telegram to Vietnam as soon as possible to inform your mother." And I request their permission to leave.

The boys stay behind while Bach takes me to visit the central part of the refugee camp. I feel like a child going to the country fair. Under the faint glow of their kerosene lamps, the fruit stands and sandal shops look appealing. Bach inquires about the price of rubber sandals. "They are not expensive," she says "but we don't have any money."

Memories of that red-hot dock and scorching sand flash through my mind. "I have a ring we could sell," I exclaim, showing it to her. Bach had given away everything she owned before leaving Vietnam. Delighted, she says we must ask Hung tonight how we could arrange to sell it. Someday, Mother, I will give you back the ring...I promise!

The light is on at the Information Center where admission is free like in a museum. As we enter, many people are milling about, chatting, and I recognize several familiar faces from our group. The room contains only a desk and a few chairs which are already taken. After a quick survey of the place, we leave because there is no worthwhile information to be had here! Our feet are drawn to the sandy path leading to the sea, but we must head back. I hesitate, for I would love to see the shining sea help the oysters capture the stars; I would gladly hide my lie in one of those jewel boxes...

On our way back, we meet Luc and Thanh. Bach tells them about our plans for the ring. Our friends have no intention of hanging onto their uncle, and I agree. We can't always be dependent on someone or be a burden to others. We come to an agreement: when we arrive in Galang, they will ask their uncle's permission to be on their own. This decision strenghthens our bonds of friendship even more – the four young fledgelings fallen from their nest will fly off together!

In the reception hall everyone is preparing a nook in which to rest their dreams. We would like to do likewise but since the place is already full, we have no choice but to spread our plastic sheet on the gravel stones near the entrance. We don't settle down to sleep right away because Hung said he would come tonight. When he arrives he gives us a snack and simply smiles gracefully. In no time, we are having a friendly conversation, eating apples and drinking soda pop. I don't talk much, for I need to savour this harmony, this juicy apple...

It is quite late by the time Hung leaves. While my brother and I exchange a few comments about him, Bach and Luc talk about a letter which Hung suggested they write to the United Nations Organization. "Aren't you children sleeping yet?" someone impatiently shouts, annoyed by our whisperings... Right away, we lie down to sleep. Thanh and Luc share one blanket; Bach and I, the other.

The wind is on patrol, chasing away the mosquitoes. Awakened by the loud snores, fireflies intercept these blood-thirsty insects. Beneath the plastic sheet, the stones are complaining that I am too heavy; and I reply that they are too hard...

Aroused by the shuffling sound of sandals at my feet, I realize that I am not at home, Bach greets me with a smile. Together we fold up our cold blanket, then walk over to the common faucet to wash our faces. Our brothers, and many others, still refuse to admit that the night is over. Down the nearby lane, Bach stops to ask a lady where the toilets are. "By the seashore, on this side", she replies, pointing with her finger. We can't find any toilets, only a long fenced-in quay jutting out to sea. It is scary to stand on these wobbly wooden planks and the height makes me dizzy. Bach tells me not to look down if I am so afraid. I have never seen toilets like these that look like belvederes.

When we return to the reception hall, everybody is up. For breakfast, we prepare some instant noodle soup and eat it in Mr. Nghi's apartment. An atmosphere of excitement suddenly permeates the air in the vast hall. Ears perk up to learn that we will be leaving for Galang this afternoon. "Hurray!!!" many cry out, and the joy becomes contagious.

Hung returns this morning with a stamped envelope for Bach and Luc. Then he and Luc leave together in search of a buyer for my ring. Mr. Nghi inquires, "Who is this nice young man, Bach?"

"A friend," she promptly replies as she settles down to write her letter. When I walk by the long table, carrying the dishes to be washed, Bach looks up at me with a grin, "Can you do them alone?"

"Of course," I nod. Thanh, who has nothing to do, is aimlessly wandering about. I am happy to be staying with Bach and Luc. Since they are older than we are, they can play the role of big sister and big brother with us.

When everything is cleaned and stored away, I go and sit out front on a bench to listen to the music coming from the next house. A lady in her sixties comes over to where I am sitting and I, of course, stand up to greet her. She sits down and starts asking me if it is true that we are leaving this afternoon. Her drab attire reminds me of a story my mother once told me, "Long, long ago. before the world of the living was separated from the immortal world, fairies would take on the form of a poor old lady to test the goodness of men."

"You're very lucky to leave so soon. My family and I are waiting..." the old lady bitterly went on to say. I ask her if she has heard of Galang and she replies "Yes. There is little water on that island, but representatives from the free nations often visit Galang. You will have a better chance of being sent to a third country from there." Heaving a deep sigh, she continues talking, as if to herself. "The longer you remain in this land of dust and heat, the less chance you have of getting a clean bill of health and the longer you must wait to be accepted somewhere."

Then she goes on to talk about Airraya. "This camp was built two years ago. When the first refugees arrived, the island was inhabited by only a few Indonesians. After having to fight off the ocean pirates, the newcomers then had to fight against famine, the weather, disease. They needed food and shelter but the Indonesians were asking exorbitant prices for rice and even for cutting down trees. A gold ring could only buy you a bowl of rice. But when more refugees arrived, they fought with the Indonesians to get trees. A tree like this one would cost the lives of two or three men," she said, her hand caressing a wooden post. "These battles and malaria decimated the people like the plague. They buried them up there near the spring, and the stream became polluted. My family arrived at that time. So I know why there is a water shortage problem. Because the refugee population kept on increasing, the United Nations Organization finally had to intervene. Since then, we have been receiving aid: food, medicine, protection. Now we have to wait for a future. Oh!, I almost forgot about the water...in the end they moved the cemetery in order to decontaminate the stream..." I gaze over the island awestruck by what has happened. In silence, we pause for a minute in remembrance of those who died before reaching the land of freedom! The first refugees paid the price for my freedom!

Bach is showing Luc the letter she just wrote. When my brother and I join them, Luc shows us the money my ring brought. Now I can buy some sandals and the rest of the money will be placed in safekeeping with Luc – he is the only one who has a pocket. After lunch, we start packing our things once again. It doesn't take long because the sum total of our possessions is: one tin cup, one bag of provisions, one sweater, one pair of shorts and one pair of slacks.

Without any regrets, we leave Airraya under the envious gaze of the other camp inmates. Greetings of "bon voyage" and "good luck" accompany us to the dock. Now that my feet are shod with rubber sandals, they are proudly crowing at the hot sand and defying the burning dock. We are boarding a boat on which Hung is a crew member. It is about thirty meters long, but they say we are to rendez-vous with another bigger boat. As the engine roars to life, the island of Airraya, with her outstretched beach, slowly recedes behind us. In the country where I want to go, there is snow. The cold winter nights might erase the image of Airraya, but I will always remember her name...

The boat is gathering speed and we all have to brace ourselves in order not to fall. Furious waves come crashing against the sides of the brazen boat, arousing my horrible companion – nausea! During a tacking maneuver, a boy is swept overboard. Hung promptly dives in to rescue him. Stark terror charges through me because there are sharks everywhere! But both swimmers manage to climb back on board, safe and sound, but soaking wet.

118

Oh yes, I can see it – a lovely big ship decked with gloss. In elegant white letters, the name *Lift Line* is written on the ship's blue hull. I once saw such a ship on television. How wonderful it will be to have a real washroom instead of a stream and a belvedered out-house. My dreams will surely change colour when I sleep in a clean white bed without any rocks under the sheet. But first I have to climb up that rope ladder which is dangling down precariously. Only a mountain climber could scale such a perilous cliff. I must concentrate on only one thing – where to place my hands and feet. What if I fall? I can still see my wild-eyed cousin and hear his distraught voice when he told us about the death of his two-year-old daughter in 1975. "I was climbing up the ship's rope ladder with my daughter in my arms. My wife was one rung above me, carrying the baby. There were lots of people on the ladder and the wind was blowing very hard. When the bombs came down, the ship was propelled away at full speed under the impact, and my daughter was snatched from my numb arm by one of the ropes..."

Finally at the top, a tall, pale-faced gentleman with a cheery smile stretches out his hand to me. As my feet touch the bridge, my mind remains blank.

We are being escorted down into the hold of the ship. I don't dare touch anything because in this civilized world, touching a button can be very dangerous. Our guide, Doctor Son, is Vietnamese. Our group must be special because this ship can accommodate thousands of passengers, and today it is making this trip for sixty-five of us. Frankly, I don't know why we are special. The room we are in looks like a big dark steel box. We will have to remain in this gloomy place for sixteen hours. "You can all settle down now. There are plenty of bamboo mats and life-jackets for everybody... Don't try to go further back into the hold. Stay here!" the doctor advises before heading up the stairs. I feel like a midget in this enormous cage. Everyone makes a dash for the mats and orange-colored vests.

Without any argument, all four of us take leave of Mr. Nghi. If my intuition is correct, I don't think he is Bach and Luc's favourite uncle. Like the others, we spread out our mats and use the life-jackets for pillows. "Sleep is the best solution when you're tired," concludes Bach before lying down. Thanh and I follow suit while our friend Luc remains sitting, lapsing into forgetfulness.

Although the sun is shining outside, the sounds of a storm are heard down here. A thundering echo is playing timpani on our steel walls, powerfully resounding to the four corners of the hold. I miss my attic, my bed, my blanket, those rainy afternoons sitting by my window... This iron floor, this pillow and this sinister room remind me that I am nothing but a refugee.

The doctor's wife comes down the stairs, arms laden with clothing. The crowd immediately surges around her and fawns her as though she were the wife of a President. Bach and I stay put because we haven't a chance to get near her. I think I know this kind woman but I just can't seem to place her. She is beautiful, and uncondescending as she give out the alms. She is a real lady. And here we are, ragged and filthy, asking for mercy like beggars.

Each family is entitled to one pre-stamped envelope. I would love to write to my family but first I must ask for help from my cousin in the United States. I have to wait for my friends to finish writing to their sister before I can borrow their pen. Through a fine trickle of ink flowing onto the paper, my emotions are cast. These black ink spots mar the blue sheet like anxiety throws gloom over my dreams. I must stop and leave a bit of space for Thanh to write too. Hopefully these few words will one day lead us to the United States, to the land of flags and flowers.

"Your letters will leave tomorrow," the doctor's wife announces as she brings in our supper, aided by two Caucasian men. One representative from each group has to go and get a box of cookies and some tea. Bach walks over with the tin cup. I can't understand why I feel so inferior to these fair-skinned people and so despicable in front of this high-society lady. I wasn't raised in an environment of self-pity, yet my heart is filled with this emotion.

As our benefactors leave, Bach's voice draws me back to our little family circle. Contrary to custom, nobody makes the sign of the cross; we simply remain silent for a moment, contemplating this manna sent from heaven.

With relish, we savor the exquisite cookies, steaming hot tea and relaxed conversation. All that is missing is the moonlight and a bit of poetry for this meal to resemble the friendly gatherings we used to enjoy at our grandparents' house long ago...

Through the gaping hole made by the staircase, the night creeps in. Even in the bowels of this ship, I sense the Indonesian sunset. The night, and the sleep it brings, chases away the melancholy in the hold. People are lining up their mats to greet the night in this cage.

I don't think I can sleep but I lie down just the same. When I made my First Communion, I had dreamed of entering the convent. Instead at the age of fifteen, I have become a handless beggar? But in life who can ever explain the "why" of things? Papa who was a wise man became the "fat fool" of the neighbourhood. It is so dark in here! I will close my eyes and try to fall asleep by counting every building on our street, right up to grandmother's house: the old hardware store, the cemetery, the tombstone shop, the Manes Temple, another cemetery, the old drugstore...

I wake up quite late, surprised to find myself in this hold. During the night, I dreamt I was a flying nun, soaring over the oceans and unfamiliar islands. I flew over the field near our home, I touched a mimosa. Like a timid young girl, the mimosa withdrew and clammed up. Then dawn arrived. "Who wants some porridge?" asks Bach. I have to shake off sleep again before replying.

This morning, some of us risk venturing further into the hold. Nothing interesting. Only row upon row of control buttons decorating the iron walls. What I would like to find is a toilet...Bach and I climb up to the bridge where lots of people have already assembled. Since neither one of us likes crowds, we wander off to our own little corner and watch the waves and islands drift by. A little girl wearing crisp new clothes and closely cropped hair comes over to talk to us. Just as I thought – she is Dr. Son's daughter. She must be lonely having no friends to play with on this big ship. We cannot respond to the little girl because our hearts are not in a playful mood. The painful separation from our loved ones, the adaptation to so many foreign places and our unpredictable future, have made us as lonely as the child. Lan (the nice lady with whom I bathed on the deck of the fishing boat) arrives, proudly displaying her new sweater. Just when the little girl is about to start up a converstaion with Lan, her mother calls her away.

Bach gets up and I traipse behind in search of our brothers. Finally we find them up on deck, hiding behind the reservoirs. Bach and Luc are now talking with members of their family. It would appear that their cousin Thanh found a solution to the compromise he made regarding the rings which were handed over to the Vietnamese officials at sea.

My bladder is about ready to burst...but I am too shy to ask where the toilet is. I am also very nervous about our landing in Galang in a few hours. What will they do about our false ages? Thanh, I am happy to note, is calmly examining each detail of the ship's construction and he doesn't seem the least bit concerned by this question.

CHAPTER 16

GALANG

We arrive in Galang around noon. This island is as green and beautiful as all the others but its concrete wharf gives it a civilized look. The Indonesian army is here to greet us. Their uniforms, complete with cartridge belts and weapons make me shiver. We are being escorted beneath the canopy of a building that resembles a sawmill. The soldiers make us sit down on woodpiles to count us – like chickens in a coop. I can relax for now because they are not asking for our names or dates of birth, yet... While we sit and wait, I survey the area. We are wedged between the forest and the ocean and it dawns on me that the camp is not close by. Bach opens the cookie box and asks if we want to eat lunch. All three of us shake our heads. If only I could find a bathroom! Drownsiness is making me yawn. This golden noonday sun reminds me of when my sister and I used to sell ice cream. Oh how we dreaded having it all melt away at noontime.

A big truck comes screeching to a halt on the rough gravel road. The Indonesians help us climb aboard. I am still feeling dizzy. First sea-sickness, now land-sickness! The vehicle stirs up gravel then veers onto a smooth asphalt road which I hadn't seen before. It forges ahead like a carrier pidgeon. The road rolls out its gray carpet cutting the immature forest in two. Winded, the truck suddenly stops at the entrance of the refugee camp. Stepping down, we carefully inspect our surroundings as though we are potential real-estate buyers. Without delay, we follow the guide who is waiting to climb up the slope with us. I try to walk faster but the earth is swaying beneath my feet. My legs refuse to obey me. Seeing us dragging our bag, the guide (a soldier) takes pity on us. Hoisting up his rifle, he makes a sign to Bach, indicating that we should let him carry it. Exhausted, we must cross over narrow boardwalks, and tread on fissured soil, jump over ditches and weave our way between long and narrow buildings that look like modern hen houses. The wind has stopped in its tracks to watch us climb every step of the way up this hill. Little by little, the sun is draining all my energy. I would love to just lie down in one of these ditches and forget about what might happen next...

Near the summit, we enter one of the long buildings. It is pitch black in here. The sun must have blinded me because at first it was black and now having recovered my sight, I see we are walking with measured tread down a narrow wooden aisle. This symmetrical structure really looks like an empty hen house. After going by a series of small cubicles surrounded by curtains, we pass between two rows of bunk beds. By the time we reach the far end of the building, there are only about ten of us remaining to be lodged. We four take over the bottom level of the very last bed. Totally worn out, I collapse on the hard wooden bed. When I close my eyes, I can hear my heart thumping and feel the sweat rolling down my back. For a long moment, all is drowned in silence, heat and fatigue. My urge to pee has passed. I know it is not healthy, but I am too tired to care.

When I open my eyes, I see that Bach has managed to borrow a pail. Yes, a good shower would do us a world of good. My head feels as empty as this dusty square bed. According to the information we were given, the spring must be near the edge of the woods. After a few minutes' walk, we come upon a group of people carrying pails and standing around a pool of water. Is that the spring? Some women are dispersing the crowd, saying, "Let them draw water first; they have just arrived." We are allowed to fill our pail from this dwindling stream without having to wait our turn.

After thanking the women for being so kind, we leave with our full pail. It is difficult to walk at a steady pace and our precious liquid is spilling out. Two young boys come up and offer to carry it for us. Along the way, we learn that the six small curtained cubicles at each end of the barracks are washrooms. How wonderful it will be to enjoy a bit of privacy at last! But you have to be careful – a gust of wind can easily lift up the shower curtain. The soap looks like an old yellow brick, but it washes everything. Our bodies are covered with rainbow-colored bubbles which unfortunately, are too fragile. They remind me of the story about the princess who wanted to have a necklace made out of these bubbles... We use our tin cup to rinse off our soapy skin with this rejuvenating water. For a facecloth, we use Bach's scarf. It seems like only yesterday I was still a little girl bathing with my mother. But today everything is changed. It is like a dream... After shaking off the excess water, we feel like exchanging clothes. So Bach puts mine on and I wear hers. It is one way to outwit poverty. "Tonight, we can wash our underclothes and we will be alright for tomorrow morning," says Bach, the practical thinker.

We have to wait for the others to finish their supper so we can borrow their pots and dishes. Luc returns with some drinking water which he found back in the forest and Thanh brings back firewood. While waiting to prepare our evening meal, we notice that some of the others have had the time to go shopping. "We'll have to go tomorrow!" Bach exclaims, still starry-eyed.

Just outside our barrack, a large rectangle of sand laid out with tin, makes up our kitchen. We dig a hole in the sand, place three rocks around it and...we have a wood stove! After cooking and eating our frugal meal, we hurry to return the borrowed articles before the sun turns to dusk. Nightfall is slowly creeping down the mountain. I see a couple who arrived here before us. They are awaiting the birth of their first child before making the voyage. Several snorers intone the overture of a nocturnal sonata as we settle down to sleep, almost worry-free and imagining Mother is there to tuck us in. Thanh and Luc cover themselves with one blanket while I wrap the other one around myself and my friend. I feel so tired, I can feel my body dissolving and molding itself to the flat, rigid form beneath me. One day, when I am too tired to go on living, they will put me in a wooden box and life will continue without me...

"You haven't forgotten what you must buy, have you? Your fineries...etc?" says Luc teasingly as he hands us a bundle of Indonesian bills. Bach and I go hopping down the steep slope which was so exhausting to climb yesterday – it is always easier to go down than up. In front of the magnificent Buddhist temple dominating the opposite mountain, we stop to admire its splendour. A rugged wooden staircase running down to the road beckons us to climb it. But I just remembered, "Where are the shops on this island?" There is only one road and it crosses the island.

"The shops must be in the center of the camp," Bach explains. Since there are no sidewalks, we stroll down the middle of the road. To our left, trees are greening their leaves in the sun. On our right, identical barracks almost overlap one another like giant fish scales strewn at the foot of the mountain. Each one is made of wood and decked with a tin roof. It looks like a peaceful little village whose sole enemy is the heat but I don't like its bevelled architecture and its forced placidity. It saddens me not to hear the familiar sounds of barking dogs, meowing alley cats, shouting merchants, creaking hammocks or a squeaky rocking chair...

The road keeps running on ahead of us...the shops are really far; I am starting to feel ravenous. Here, the camp's features are starting to change: a white Red Cross tent and two deserted hospitals blankly stare at each other in disgust over this island's recent past of violence and poverty. Up ahead there is a sign which says: CENTRE COMMERCIAL. "What is this?" I ask, and Bach explains that it is a shopping center. Is this possible! A marketplace like the one in Saigon, with its hundreds of shiny fruits which I always craved for but could never afford? But Bach keeps on walking past it and I follow. She seems to know where to find what we need.

I keep my eyes peeled, making sure nobody touches us because I know from experience that although money has no wings, it can easily fly away into someone else's pocket. After careful inspection, we manage to find a merchant who is selling underwear – a young woman whose basket contains just three pairs of panties and two bras. When Bach is told the price of these items, she immediately withdraws her hand from the basket as if she had just touched a hot iron. Such prices could quickly burn up all our money! Unfortunately, nobody else is selling this type of clothing, so my friend has to try to bargain her down. But this woman knows exactly what to say in order to maintain her price while convincing us to buy. Pondering and hesitant, Bach holds the two panties poised in her hand for quite some time before paying for them.

Then we enter the General Store. One of the clerks speaks both Vietnamese and Chinese. We ask her for a mosquito net, a plastic pail, four bowls and four spoons. Also, a roll of toilet paper. "Every month, a woman needs this," Bach whispers in my ear and I understand only too well. After paying for these items, we are left with nothing but small change. This means we will still have to borrow cooking pots!... We must set up a schedule so that we don't always bother the same people. The three men sleeping in the bed next to ours stop to inquire about the cost of our purchases. According to them, women are much better bargainers; yet we thought the prices were fixed.

We arrive at the barracks exhausted but happy, because today we will be eating supper from our own dishes. Like the peaceful flowers on the tree standing in our schoolyard, we are slowly settling into our new life. Happiness is like one of those sunny flowers that blooms one day and withers the next. Together, we are as happy as newlyweds. Luc and Bach have become a real brother and sister to us and they love us more than anyone else on the island. Also, we have the greatest respect for them. Together we form a small utopian society where each task is performed according to everyone's preference and ability. So even if water is scarce and our ration for rice is dwindling, we never suffer from hunger, thirst, or uncleanliness. The rain will fall down on us, a new ration of food will come and the hearts of generous souls will once again be touched.

Tonight, on the eve of our first weekend in Galang, our barrack has a funereal complexion. A young couple share their oil lamp with us. These are made out of empty tin cans. Most of the young people are gathered around our bed chatting together. I find it so interesting to listen to this idle talk, for it reminds me of those nights when the neighbourhood children would take advantage of the blackouts to tell each other frightful stories on the street corners. I can still remember how our laughter used to startle the policemen. "Don't be so gross!" shouts Thanh, Bach's cousin, to my brother when he attempts to spit through the open window.

I know he didn't spatter the bed on purpose, but I have to play my motherly role. "You could at least excuse yourself, Thanh," I exclaim in a scolding voice. To my great surprise, he jumps off the bed, grabs his shirt and bolts outside, fuming. Embarrassed by his reaction, I want to strike out at him...

"Leave him alone," my big sister advises. In silence, I try to hide my fury but all I can think of is how to punish my brother. In my opinion, he deserves to be knelt in a corner, nose to the wall, have his ears pinched, a few hairs pulled and his bottom spanked. Perhaps after that, he might repent!

When everyone retires for the night, Bach tries to console me, saying, "Thanh shouldn't have screamed like that...he didn't want to embarrass you but he has his pride. Between brothers and sisters, it is often difficult to accept the other's opinion. It happens to us too, you know!" My anger melts into tears as Bach gives me a knowing grin.

Together we start putting up the mosquito netting, but Thanh is not back yet. We go out looking for him all the way around the barrack, but he is nowhere to be found. Back inside, we wait. Luc borrows a flashlight and sets out to look for him too. I am getting worried. Where could he be? My friends try to comfort me but it is no use. After a while Luc returns alone. Since we don't know the island, he doesn't think it is wise to venture any further. All the more reason for me to worry! Yet my friends aren't panicking. "Let's get some sleep and worry tomorrow," Bach suggests. The two of us sleep under the netting while Luc wraps himself up in a blanket on the next bed with the men. That surprises me but I realize that for centuries, people have always made fun of boys and girls who sleep in the same bed. And where is my brother sleeping tonight? It is already late and the whole barrack is asleep while I remain wide-eyed, scrutinizing the darkness and wrestling with my nightmares: Thanh fell in a ditch and broke his leg; he was bitten by a snake or a scorpion; the Indonesians captured him; or maybe he drowned in a pool of water...

At daybreak, I wake up to find Thanh sitting at the foot of my bed. I think I am seeing a ghost! His presence brings in a whiff of cool night air. I am so happy to see that he is out of danger that I don't even bother asking where he spent the night. I will let Bach and Luc reprimand him. But to my surprise, they simply ask, "Where did you spend the night?" as if he had just come back from a trip. Embarrassed, Thanh replies looking sheepish, "In the church," as though he expected a scolding. As of today, I have decided to entrust my brother to their care.

Today is Sunday. Last night's event is already forgotten and we are all getting back to our daily routine. I know this barrack inside and out by now: 24 bunk beds lined up in two rows, 6 washrooms surrounded by coloured curtains at each end of the long aisle, and a narrow corridor crossing the barrack midway. I also know almost everyone by name. But what good does that do me? I am still searching for something which I don't have and that isn't here! I find the weather is sultry and gray, despite the blowing wind and dazzling sunshine.

As I empty out the dishwater into the ditch behind the barrack, the noonday sun hammers my head, shortening my shadow on the ground. Two women approach me (probably sisters) asking, "Is this the newcomers' barrack?" An irresistable urge to burst out laughing grips me because they remind me so much of the Dupont detectives in "Tintin". They also inquire about my trip. One after the other, they keep interrogating me; it is almost like standing in front of a judge.

"Did you change your age on your records? one of them asks with a persistent look."

"Yes," I reply, like the accused before the court.

"By how many years?" the other continues, acting like a defense counsel.

"Four years."

"How old are you?"

"Fifteen."

"Have you met the U.N.O. representatives?"

"No, we've only been here four days."

"They won't believe you're only eleven."

"This could delay your departure, you know. You'll soon find out that you have to go through countless interviews and the medical examinations are endless."

"Will I have to stay on this island much longer?" I ask resignedly.

"Some stay here as long as two years, sometimes longer. But you're young and you must have a clean medical record. Lately the representatives have been coming here regularly. Last year there were over 20,000 refugees in this camp; now half of them are gone. So don't worry!"

After a moment of reflection, I decide to ask the question that has been haunting me for so long: "What would happen if I told them the truth about my age?"

"That would only create more problems. You have no papers to prove your real age, so don't try to complicate matters further."

And off they go, smiling, entering our barrack to continue their tour. They stop near our bed to speak to Bach and Luc. Waiting for them to leave, I rinse out my clean dishes

130

once again. Deep inside me a burning rage makes me want to scream in self-defense. I hate these women! I can't wait to get out of this camp, but I am not anxious to face the immigration tribunal. What punishment do they reserve for those who lie? I will be miserable for the rest of my life if the hope which my family has placed in me is forever buried beneath the rubble of dishonesty. Lord, you who were prepared to save the city of Sodom in the name of five honest men, please save me for the love of my honest and upright family!

All afternoon I remain cloaked in silence. Nobody knows that I am desperately trying to break down the prison walls and escape the quagmire created by my false age. I am wrestling against windmills like Don Quixote... It was also on a Sunday that Father Sinh – my father's friend and translator of the book "Don Quixote de la Mancha" – came to our house with his work, I was nine years old when I learned about this character with a wild imagination... Unfortunately time has left its mark, both on the translator of this book and on its young reader; he is now in a concentration camp and I, in a refugee camp! Injustice tortures the just, while justice condemns the unjust. At times, life has the bitter aftertaste of an unripened fruit.

Now that supper is over, we are all getting ready to go to church. Luc went to borrow someone's trousers – I didn't know boys are as vain as girls. Lighthearted and serene, forgetting who and where we are, we trudge down the road. The church is even farther than the marketplace; it is sitting on top of a hill covered with crushed stone. All the lights come on and everyone rises just as we are about to enter. Since our clothes aren't very clean, we remain in the back pews.

The wooden benches, the hymns, the sermon...they all remind me of my parish in Vietnam. When I walk back up the aisles after communion, I suddenly recognize two familiar faces: they were members of our parish. I must go over and talk to them after mass. What a joy to see some of my compatriots, even though they were among those who spoke in derogatory terms about my family.

Glancing over to my right, I notice a small vestibule – that must be where my brother slept last night. After the ite missa est, everyone walks out in silence and I scrutinize this indifferent crowd in search of the boy and girl I knew from home. I smile to them in recognition but they don't respond – their new shirts and jeans create a barrier betweeen us.

As I turn to walk out behind Bach, Luc and Thanh, I realize just how precious they are to me. We stop for a moment to pray at the foot of the Blessed Virgin. I feel so worn out and tortured with remorse for having lied about my age.

When the last people leave their pews, genuflecting and signing themselves, the chapel is closed down for the night cloaked in silence and darkness. Down the hill, our camp looks like a cemetery where tombstones are devoid of crosses. I am in a cold sweat just thinking that we will be sleeping at the far end of the camp, near the sinister shades of night.

As we head down the road, somehow the path seems longer and quite different in the darkness. The wooden huts near the shopping center have been transformed into poetic cafés where lovers are lost in contemplation of their happiness, while other lonely souls build dreams amid the blend of cigarette smoke and coffee aroma.

Along the way, only the smiles and sundries sold by the cigarette and dream merchants are illuminated by the faint lamps' glow. In the darkness of night, we finally reach the last slope leading to our barrack. A gentle breeze cools our sweating bodies but also jolts our nostrils with the nauseating stench of garbage. I remain impassive, holding my breath, for I remember what my mother once told me when I had pinched my nose near a garbage truck, "When you die, you won't smell any better!" she had said.

Once inside the barrack, Luc and Thanh prepare to fetch some water but we are told that the small springs are dry and that access to the larger one up on the mountain is forbidden. It is constantly being guarded. Any violation of this warning could result in a delay of the offenders' departure date. Without water we can do nothing, but we certainly don't want to risk prolonging our stay on this island. Let's hope it rains soon. We happen to know that our neighbour – sleeping two beds away from us and who has been here for quite some time – has a big water reservoir out on the verandah, near the window. Forgetting that we have just returned from mass, we decide to steal some of this water. But we have to wait until everybody is asleep. When the whole barrack is finally busy chasing dreams, Luc and Thanh sneak out with a pail and creep down the verandah in their bare feet. The gurgling water doesn't waken anyone but it makes my heart beat wildly for what seems like an eternity. Only when Luc is securely tucked in the next bed and I am lying beneath the netting between Thanh and Bach does it finally calm down.

Days and nights drag by. When the sun sets, we go to bed and we get up when it rises. At midday, the warm breeze invites us to siesta. The waiting is torture. We still don't seem to be moving any closer to our goal.

Le Du comes over to inform me that he has sent a telegram to Vietnam. I thank him since I couldn't have done it myself; I have no more money. I can't even be glad because he also reminds me of the debt my mother has to repay or that I must repay by asking for my cousin's help. But until I hear from him, there is nothing I can do.

Mr. Nam – the man who had told me during the voyage that we were heading for Singapore – has been appointed our barrack representative. This week Luc, Thanh and the others accompany him to collect our food supplies. Three hours later the boys return, exhausted and perspiring. Yet they don't want us to help them the next time. Each person receives one bag of rations for eight days. According to the words on the bags, these provisions are provided by the United Nations Organization. In great haste, we open our plastic bags to see what humanity has sent us. There are two kilos of rice, canned meat, beans, spinach, fish, tea bags, sugar, salt and red peppers. Carefully, we place our treasures underneath the bed. It is as though Santa Claus has come by.

Now that our food supply problem is settled, each day we manage to find a minimum of water by wringing out every last drop from the rocks. But other sorts of problems arise daily. My brother's two pairs of shorts are worn out and Luc only has one pair. After counting and recounting the loose change we have left, Bach seems to think we have enough to buy at least a metre of material to make new ones. In fact, it turns out that we have enough not only for material, but thread, needles, zippers and a bar of soap as well. Bach is an excellent seamstress and we all pitch in to help with the hand sewing. Together we produce three pairs of shorts: one pair each for Luc, Thanh and myself. Also, since the pregnant lady gives us some old clothes that were discarded by those who have already left the camp, we now have enough to wear, both day and night.

After all these weeks, I finally get to know who the captain of our boat was. His name is Mr. Cap, one of the three men sleeping in the bed next to ours. He and his friends are like the Three Musketeers. Hung, the monkish young man who had cooked rice on deck during our journey at sea, informs us that on the fifth night, we had been completely lost. Everyone seems to hold this against Mr. Cap but I think he did his best and nothing terrible happened. The captain told us that during the voyage his food had been prepared with powdered soap, by mistake, instead of flour. Today he seems to find the incident very amusing.

The barrack is generally very quiet, like a living room, whereas the kitchen area is the meeting place for sharing stories, jokes and the tragic comic situations we have had to contend with. Among the sixty-five people in our group, there are only six women. The men have to cook their own meals. I will never forget the time when Le Du's brothers were trying to prepare a dessert. It so happened that the salt and sugar bags looked identical, and unfortunately they used the wrong one!

The kind gentleman who had sheltered me from the rain, beneath his raincoat up on deck during the crossing, is called Minh. He is now cooking his soup nearby and teasing me. "Young lady, your sweater is orange! But it wasn't that color when you tucked yourself under my arm to sleep the other day... No, no don't say anything. I know that I smelled awful that day because some clumsy rogues had spilled four

litres of fish brine all over me." I find his mimicry very funny
and it reminds me of my uncle who used to clown around with
us. In my country, it is customary to address every man over
the age of thirty with the word "uncle", but these men want
me to call them "brother", like I do with Luc. I find that embarrassing.

One day we discovered that lice were starting to nestle
in our hair. It was almost an epidemic but we managed to
make them all disappear. I even wished I had more so Bach
could play in my hair for a longer time. My mother never had
time for that, and I hated lice so much because people would
keep away from me when I had them.

For over two weeks now we have been camped on this
island like nomads. We listen carefully every time a voice
crackles over the loudspeaker to call out the names of those
who must go to the office for an interview. This morning
when we hear our boat's number being called out, the shrieks
of joy almost bring the barrack down. The echo repeats it two
or three times. Everybody gets dressed, combs his hair, scur-
ries to find his sandals...The problem of my age starts tor-
menting me again. I don't know whether to be happy or
worried..."Now, Doan, you're not alone to face this
problem!" I tell myself.

The office is a bit past the church, down the road leading to the beach I am told. Already I am dragging my feet,
feeling weak from the heat, so weak that I just want to stop
and rest.

A large crowd is waiting when we arrive. The Interview-
ing Committee's office looks like a white mobile trailer
suspended in mid-air and supported by wooden posts. We
wait our turn like everyone else. People are talking about
their voyage: storms, pirates, being lost...But to me, nothing
seems more tragic than the upcoming interview. They will
laugh at me, or get angry...they might even lock me up.

At last it is our turn. My brother and I are sitting in the
office of a young Caucasian, assisted by a Vietnamese interpreter. They are smiling at us and writing down the names
and ages of all the members of my family – which I give them,

keeping in mind our false ages – expecting to be declared a liar any minute now. But they simply conclude the interview by asking which country we would like to go to. I timidly reply that we have a cousin in the United States but that we are prepared to go to any country that will have us.

Although I know they can't kill us, I still dread the final interview. About ten days later, our group is called to the Health Center to be X-rayed. The Indonesian handling the machine indicates that I should remove my shirt. Blushing profusely, I acquiesce to his request. Oh, life can sometimes be so cruel and indifferent to our fears. I guess one must be prepared to pay the price of humiliation to find happiness in the promised land.

Even though the earth keeps on turning, time remains at a standstill in this barrack. According to the lunar calendar, the New Year is about to begin. In Vietnam, everybody is celebrating. Over the past few years, this feast had lost some of its gaiety. But we would still celebrate it to remind us of happier times. To express their friendship, families would exchange small gifts such as a chicken, a watermelon, oranges, a bottle of wine or a box of candies. This feast is a celebration of family unity. But no more does New Year's have meaning for us. Tonight we sit around quietly waiting for the old year to end. It is the first time I fully understand that I am without a country and without a family. The feeling of being severed from all tradition is very painful.

The moon never shows its face on this last day of the year. In the open fire, a succession of exploding food cans (which were past their expiry dates) imitate the traditional sound of the midnight bugles. We try to sleep, thinking that tomorrow there will be no blessing, no greeting, no gifts, no visitors... Nothing but mediocrity and boredom. I wish I could dream that tomorrow the sky will be peacefully blue, that a good fairy will bring back the sunshine to ripen the rice and at day's end, trace a moon in the sky. If wine had the power to transport me back home I would gladly drink it and then capture the intoxicating effects of the red remains of the firecrackers.

I wonder if Father found out why we are no longer there? Will Mother have to threaten to set the house on fire, as she did last New Year's Day, to force him to come out of his corner? Where will my family go visiting today and who will visit them, since my mother has no money for presents?

The night is long...as long as my grandmother's white hair, discolored by years of war and famine. Even though the year has changed its name, life goes on just as quietly as ever. Morning comes and the flowers drink up the dew while our neighbor, Mr. Ba, fills his ailing lungs with fresh air. The four of us are still on the best of terms but we keep our thoughts to ourselves for fear of burdening the others.

When the night is warm, people gather round in the yard to chat, often forgetting bedtime. Sometimes the moon gazes down at us while we reminisce and tell sad and funny stories that make me wet my pants, and occasionally my eyes. When someone starts to tell an obscene joke, Luc always gets up and says, "It's time to go to bed, children!" He reminds me of my father who always hated this type of story. Once when it wasn't even dark out yet, Luc used his usual phrase when someone started to tell an off-color joke. As punishment, we forced him to tell us the story of Dracula – whom he imitates extremely well.

As an added surprise, there is a nice green cabbage in our food supplies this week. This will be a welcome substitute for the beans which have become the island's main staple. We have also been given two litres of kerosene but it is quite a problem to find containers for it. Thanks to this black gold, my brother is no longer a nobody – he has invented a new type of oil lamp which he makes out of empty tin cans. This means we often have to eat beans to supply him with cans. I am a bit wary of his invention but everyone else thinks he is very ingenious. At first his lamps were comprised of two wicks; now his latest model has six. I must admit that the barrack is well lit up...and black with smoke too! The fact that Bach and Luc don't say a word to him about his hazardous creations annoys me. On the other hand, for the moment, it is the only exciting thing he has found to do on this island. And if I tell him that what he is doing is dangerous, he might run away again. When I saw the gaping hole burnt in Mr. Nghi's shower curtain, I checked his wicks and told Bach about it. She simply smiled. I am stunned by her nonchalant reaction.

The days drag by so slowly. All we do is eat, sleep and wait. There is no privacy here whatsoever. When we climb up the hill with a pail of water, everybody knows we are going to the bathroom. And where can I hide while I mend my underwear? I guess I haven't been exposed to enough poverty because I cannot rid myself of old inhibitions.

In order to give meaning to our waiting game, we decide to register for an English class. We must first complete a classification test, and that makes me nervous because at school I always did poorly in that subject. The school is composed of several barracks. A charming lady invites me into her office and I smile to disguise my fear.

"Hello, how are you? she says in a solemn tone as if I were entering the White House".

"Yes...uh...fine!"

"What's your name?" she asks, still unsmiling.

"...Doan"

"How old are you?"

I repeat her question and say the first number that comes to mind. She seems surprised but continues the interview with a long sentence that leaves me confused and shivering. I can't tell if she is an American or Vietnamese.

"That's all right. You will be in group C".

During the days that follow, I am completely engrossed in my studies. My first lesson begins with, "When I was a little girl..."

After five long weeks of this humdrum existence, the monotony is finally broken when all the young people without parents are called to the immigration office. We still have no idea what our future will be, and it becomes harder to bear when we think of our families who are depending on us for help. Will this interview be the last?

Our interviewer is a distinguished lady who is assisted by a young male interpreter. After stubbing out her cigarette, she points to a bench facing her. Like two birds on a branch, we sit down trembling, for we know she will be asking how old we are.

"She doesn't believe you..."

The interpreter's words are like a slap in the face. I feel as though I have been struck down by a thunderbolt. Tongue-tied with fear, I finally manage to mumble something. Then the lady changes the subject asking in what country we would like to be relocated. To the United States? My cousin never answered my letters, so good-bye to that country which reminded me all too much of the war anyway! To France? Its leftist government scares me. To West Germany? The Berlin wall is too scary... Finally, we choose to go to Canada because of its reputation as pacifist nation.

The interview is over and I run out of the office to get away from this lady who holds the key to our future in her briefcase. During the days that follow, I am haunted by the conviction that they are checking up on our false birth dates.

The weather has turned to rain. Perhaps the sky is crying over our fate? Its warm tears are silently slithering down the leaves and pounding loudly on the roof top. The damp, glistening eyes of those I meet are sad and homesick. Some inmates are starting to receive letters and gifts from their relatives already abroad. Our friends have just received a second letter from their sister in West Germany and I am very happy for them but sad for my brother and myself. Since no mail can go directly from Indonesia to Vietnam, Bach suggests I write to my mother through her sister. I must make an effort to curb my tongue in order not to call my cousin an ungrateful traitor.

Today the couple which occupied the second bed down from ours is leaving for the United States with their newborn baby. Everybody wishes them Bon Voyage, yet we are all a little envious.

We gradually stop attending our English classes. If only I knew what language I will be speaking?

One of the boys in our group has just found a shortcut to the beach. Instead of following the road, we simply cross over the mountain next to our barrack. It isn't safe to wander off alone on this land of reptiles but the scathing heat and wide open sea beckons us daily.

Hand in hand, Bach and I walk, run and jump into this saltwater which washes away all our cares. The sea is a capricious maiden; she can be calm or turbulent, sometimes cool and distant and at other times, warm and loving. The waves are like pirates unloading their stolen treasures on the seashore. But what is the use of amassing treasures without those you love? Pretty, empty seashells have opened their butterfly wings but they can never fly. Where do the starfish come from, I wonder? Are they shooting stars that fall into the ocean last year? Like me, the tiny pebbles on this beach seem to be dreaming of their native soil. And I miss my family. My eyes scan the horizon wistfully searching for a ship that might be bringing them to me but I see only a blue expanse mirroring the sky. At high tide, the rocky cliffs bathe their feet in the water, and at low tide, hide them in the sand. I wonder what they are waiting for and what I am waiting for, standing here with tear-filled eyes. Will someone ever come and rescue us?

Quite often we sit under a shady fruitless tree to dry off our feet. Sometimes we watch the Indonesian fishermen digging up hundreds of tiny crabs along the beach. Legend has it that these creatures are the reincarnation of a young man who is searching for his lost pearl in order to learn the language of the animal kingdom. We are all searching for a universal something which we have lost. Like these grains of sand which remain side by side, we always try to do it alone never joining hands.

One day, when the tide was coming in, I almost drowned. Luckily Mr. Minh immediately jumped in and brought me back safely to shore. Since then, I call him my whale and he nicknamed me the white-nosed fox – because of the sunburns that have flayed my nose. To ease the pain in my heart, I am tempted to call him papa.

When a borrowed guitar makes its appearance in our barrack, I watch the atmosphere change. Cradled against the hearts of charming guitarists, the instrument sings out passionately on hot dreary days, interrupting the woeful crickets' song and lulling my brother to sleep on the verandah.

At night when it gets cooler, Luc borrows the guitar to accompany his sister out in the yard. We all gather round to listen to them. Bach's voice soars up like a kite in the sky or comes falling down like an autumn leaf. The notes fly off, pirouetting over the clothesline. In the still of night everybody listens, lost in his own reverie. She sings of love, of a love that hurts. One song is about two lovers who, separated by the ocean of stars overhead, could only see each other once a year in July, when the crows join their wings to form a bridge. The torrential rains that fall during the month of July are these lovers' tears. For my part, I know how to cry but I am not sure I know how to love. Dreams are pink, but reality is dull and gray. If only the future could be as poetic as a love song!

One night as I am standing outside near the barrack, Mr. Hao makes a sign for me to come to the door. He brings me into a dark corner and shoves a piece of cloth in my hand saying, "I found this on the beach. Keep it, my dear, you need it." He leaves before I have the chance to thank him. When I walk over to look at my gift beneath the lamplight, my face turns red as a beet: it is a pair of panties! Someone is coming so I hide them under the blanket. It is Mr. Cap – he hands me a poem, saying, "Read it. I wrote it for you," and before I can ask for an explanation, he is gone. The poem resembles Bach's songs. I am shaking with embarrassment because never before has a man addressed me like this. I go out on the verandah to find Mr. Cap and hand him back the poem, without saying a word.

In total confusion and frustration over everything that has happened to me tonight and feeling sorry for myself, I head straight to bed instead of going back out to listen to my friends' music-making. Tears come streaming down my face and into my ears. I just hate being a girl! I don't need a lover, or panties for that matter! If only I had a father who could say to me, "Don't be afraid, I am here. Don't worry about having lied about your age. You did the right thing, daughter." And I sob like a baby.

Mr. Cap comes over to the foot of my bed. In the darkenend barrack and to the sound of the distant guitar, he kisses me like a man kisses a woman. My cold and indifferent body turns to stone. What shall I do? Oh, I hate you; I hate men! I will never marry! He leaves me to brood in silence. Men are almost all the same. The other night on my way back from church I lost track of Mr. Minh, and a young man offered to accompany me back to camp. But half-way back, he put his hand in mine, then on my shoulders. Luckily, before anything else could happen, I arrived at the barrack crying and feeling disgusted with myself...

My sobs wake up everybody. Bach's cousin Dinh runs over to get her. Out on the verandah she wipes away my tears while I tell her what has happened. I feel bad for causing her so much trouble. When will I ever leave this island?

During the third week of March, a large number of people from our group are again called to the immigration office. The torment over my false age starts all over again. After waiting in line for hours we finally meet with the Canadian representative. He is a tall, friendly man with brown curly hair, who takes the time to smile at us before opening his files. Here comes the question of our ages...again! I feel so ashamed to have to lie to this kind man. But rather than being annoyed over my dishonesty, he gives me an affectionate look. That really surprises me! Through his interpreter he asks many questions about our family, our trip, our studies, etc. He also wants to know if we like French and the cold climate. "Yes," we answer without any hesitation, although we know nothing about either. Then he closes his file and talks for a while with the interpreter.

"Well, children, you will be future Canadians; Quebecers to be more precise. And that's not all. Mr. Ben would like to take you out to dinner tomorrow. He wants to arrange for your sponsorship into the country and will discuss this with his wife. Here is his business card, with his address and telephone number where he can be reached."

With a twinkle in his eye, the interpreter congratulates us as we sit there, paralyzed with joy. I simply can't believe that we will soon have a father who will help us resolve the dilemma of our false ages... Before leaving the office, the interpreter apologizes to Mr. Ben for taking so much time to explain things to us. After introducing himself as Mr. Huân, he informs us that his family will be leaving for Canada in a few days. "We will leave you our cooking utensils and tomorrow afternoon, I will come to pick you up. I know my wife and three daughters would love to meet you."

Having expressed our deepest gratitude to them, we immediately run over to our friends to share the good news. They are very happy for us but they are also worried about their dossiers which haven't been processed yet by the German Immigration. "Come to Canada with us!" I exclaim spontaneously. "We'll think about it; actually, the Wall scares me too," replies Bach, while Luc nods his head, pensively.

The next day, Mr. Huân accompanies us to our rendezvous. On the steps leading to the Buddhist temple, Mr. Ben has his picture taken with us. Everybody is staring as though we are a prince and princess, because we are about to acquire a Canadian father (and also because every white man on this island is looked upon with kingly respect). After a tiring trek beneath the blazing sun, we enter the camp's only restaurant. Drinks and soup are promptly served. Nervousness has taken the edge off our hunger but we know that Mr. Ben is trying to please us. Both men are quietly talking in English. Mr. Ben often glances over at us and I respond with a timid grin. I can tell, from my brother's inertia, that he is just as intimidated as I am. I just can't understand why this Canadian loves us so much. Up until now, very few people have been moved by my family's story.

"Why are you always smiling like that?" he asks me, through his interpreter.

I wanted to reply that it is my only possession but I was afraid it might offend him. So I simply said, "I don't know." At the end of the meal, he reiterates his intentions to sponsor us and informs us that he will be returning to Galang shortly. We try to show our appreciation in every way we possibly can.

Both men return to the office and we head back to our barrack alone, I feel so uncomfortable in the skin of an eleven-year-old girl. It was a terrible mistake to make myself four years younger, but how can I undo it now?

A few days later, the Huân family is preparing to leave. The interpreter's wife gave us her small oil stove, a frying pan, a cooking pot and some used clothing. I offered to help carry their luggage down to the port, and en route, after asking me my age, Mr. Huan says, "That's your age for Canada, is it?" These words certainly don't make me feel any better.

The afternoon drags on mournfully as we impatiently wait for the boat to come in. Those who are leaving are anxious to discover their new country, whereas I can't wait to share the juicy orange Mrs. Huân gave me with my brothers and sister.

Now that we have a stove, a pan, some sugar and oil, Bach plans to make donuts for Easter. In order to buy the missing ingredients, flour and eggs, we have to sell a portion of our rice. We didn't celebrate Têt but we won't miss celebrating Holy Week. We are no longer Vietnamese but we are still Christians. The boys only attend the official services but Bach and I, who are perhaps more pious, spend several hours in the chapel. On Good Friday, we fast like real adults – no food, no water and we retire early to bed. At midnight, when we get up to take a snack, the people who are awakened around us start to laugh at how seriously we fasted.

We are always busy doing something, yet the days seem as pointless and desolate as the crickets' song. I can't wait to get news from Mr. Ben. Today Bach and Luc are scheduled for an interview with the Canadian Immigration officials. I go along with them in the hope of seeing Mr. Ben, but he is not there. A cold chill runs up my spine when I hear the

American representatives interrogating a few boys from our group about their real ages. When will my turn come?

Hopelessly fed up of trying to write to my cousin, I have decided to write a letter to Mr. Ben instead, in Vietnamese. It starts like this: Dear Papa..." Then I seal the envelope and take it to the post office myself, without telling anyone about it.

Even in my sleep, I wait for an answer. I dream that he comes to get us with suitcases filled with clothing which we leave behind for our friends. Cloaked in happiness, we depart with our new father who loves us even though we are fourteen and fifteen instead of ten and eleven.

The invisible clock of the universe is marking the monotony of time with its perpetual tick-tocks. Everyone seems to be wrapped up in his own private and gloomy thoughts. This morning when I wakened, Bach had already left for mass. Later on in the afternoon, Luc takes all three of us up to the nearby hill where he tries to explain that our troubles are far from over – theirs with their relatives and mine with men. What would we do if they were to leave first and we were left on our own? Wordlessly, we watch the sun go down as we ponder our problems, letting the clinging flies feast on our bodies. For more than two months we have been eating out of the same pot and drinking from the same cup. Our fraternal bond is now even stronger than friendship.

Each day I go over to the hospital to check the posted list of names of people scheduled for a check-up. This morning I am pleased to find my name on the list.

I meet one of the girls from my school who disappeared six months before I left. I never expected to see anyone from my old life on this island. The voyage has transformed her from a school child into a young lady, but her eyes are still as playful as before. Together we talk about our recent experiences and share our hopes for the future. Loan is alone and waiting to join her father in the United States.

"Since he has already remarried, I'm not sure he'll want me there," she concludes in a sad voice.

I also learn from her that the distinguished lady I met on the Lift Line ship is our French teacher's sister, and that Mrs. Chu, our biology professor, is here in Galang.

"Let's go and pay her a visit," I say enthusiastically. And so we exchange barrack numbers before parting.

The following morning, my brother and I join the long line of people queuing outside the hospital. The sun is beating down on us so strongly that we end up having to squat on the ground. Mr. Cap walks over to talk to me; his presence makes me terribly nervous. Men are cruel and they don't understand the meaning of our silence. But not knowing what will happen during the medical examination worries me more than anything else.

When there are only some thirty people ahead of us, I realize that we are waiting to undergo a urine analysis. Seeing me empty-handed, the lady next to me advises, "Go and get a small plastic bag; the toilets are over there. Hurry up, I will keep your place for you." Thanking her, I pass on the message to my brother who dashes off to our barrack to empty out two bags of salt. It is a good thing my nervousness makes me want to pee.

After the urine test, comes the complete physical. My brother stands in line with the men, and I with the women. Mr. Cap is still hanging around me. After a long wait, I walk into a room with four other women. The nurse tells us to strip off all our clothes and to present ourselves, one after the other, in front of three doctors (two Vietnamese and one white) who are sitting on the other side of the screen. If they had sent me to the guillotine, I couldn't have been more scared than I am now. Is this a new scientific method to determine how old you are? My hands tremble as I unbutton my blouse. Oh Mother, I am sure it would have pained you too much to let us go if you had known what kinds of humiliations we would have to go through! The impatient nurse is making us hurry, jostling us like animals into the stable. I am third in line. Be brave, Doan! Christ was also naked on the cross... The white doctor examines me while the other two act as interpreters. Standing there, naked in front of three

146

men, I really have to concentrate hard to answer their questions.

After putting my clothes back on, I just stand there with a stupified look on my face. They never asked me my age! If Bach had been there, I would have opened the floodgate of my tears to release all my tension. I hope I don't meet Mr. Cap at the door. No, he has gone. I immediately rush over to join my brother.

Back at the barrack, I crawl into my solitary shell, busying myself with the humdrum routine. Still no news from Mr. Ben and no letter from my cousin. Memory is such a fragile thing! All of a sudden, Son, one of the boys, shouts to me, "You've received a registered letter." I am overjoyed by this news. Mr. Ben must have sent us our passports, or maybe my cousin in America sent us some money! Everybody shares our excitement. Luc puts on his shirt saying he will get the letter which is making me so happy that I even forgot to run over and get it myself. I feel giddy and exhilarated with happiness.

Luc arrives. He hands a letter to Bach and to me he says – "Sorry, someone else in the camp has the same name as you... Anyway, my sister wrote to all four of us." I try to hide my disappointment but the tears come gushing down like lava from a volcano. Son feels guilty for having raised my hopes so high, and I make an effort to smile at him. On this godforsaken island, one must learn to forgive.

Our friends' sister enclosed a ten dollar bill with her letter so that all four of us could buy some new clothes. "After all, we can't arrive in America dressed like beggars, can we!" Bach explains teasingly. Together, we spend the next three days in the camp's sewing room, measuring, designing, cutting and sewing. Then we borrow an iron from an ingenious gentleman – he made it out of a can of sardines filled with sand. Here we are, all dressed up in our new clothes like mannequins in a shop window, just waiting to be bought.

More endless hours of not knowing whether to be sad or happy. How will we earn our living and provide for our families in Vietnam? What language will we speak? What are we going to do about our ages?

CHAPTER 17

GOOD-BYE GALANG

This is the last time the mountains, the barracks, the road and the inmates will hear our names blasted over the loudspeakers. We will be leaving in two days and now they are calling us to sign some immigration papers at the hospital. After my brother and I stand in line for a while, we walk in. The Vietnamese secretary checks our names and birth dates, eyeing us with indifference. Then he makes us sign the paper and hands us a ticket, adding, "You will receive a bag at the Red Cross tent."

In the office facing the tent, some Indonesians are silently working and chewing gum. We are glad that our days of waiting are over. The island of Galang is sparkling under the sun and in our eyes. Everything becomes beautiful again when it no longer belongs to us. "Thanh, let's be extremely nice to Bach and Luc during these last few days. And do be careful how you act in front of people," I say to him in a burst of joy. For the first time, he agrees with me without comment.

For the remaining part of the day, all the activity is centered around our bed. Everybody, even the barrack's representative, comes over to say "Bon Voyage" to the first two from our boat to be chosen. Le Du also extends his best wishes without mentioning a word about my debt to him.

Next morning, the three men from the adjacent bed invite our foursome out to the café to celebrate our departure. Mr. Cap's presence doesn't bother me anymore because in two days, my life will be changed. Sitting here in front of a glass of juice, I can't help but recall the hours that preceded our departure from Vietnam.

The day looks bleak. Gray clouds cover the sun, the leaves are turning their backs to us and the wind is fighting with the clothesline. Our suitcase is ready. We have given our friends some of the articles which we received in the Red Cross bag (towels, soap, toothpaste, yard goods, etc...)

Bach bought us a loaf of bread and a can of condensed milk for the trip to Singapore. We are so eager to taste freedom and happiness that we have no regrets about leaving.

Now it is raining. Gusty winds are blowing in, carrying the scent of exhalations from the soil which has been parched for days. The storm is starting to blanch the valley where our camp lies. Everyone is immobilized indoors on this tearful afternoon. My friends are faithfully reading their English books. My brother is sleeping on the next bed, where idle flies are busy licking their spidery legs. I am sitting with my chin propped on the window sill, watching the air bubbles float on the water in the nearby ditch.

At nightfall, the rain clouds drift away from the island. All the youngsters in our barrack invite us out to the café. As we go skating down the muddy slopes and streets, the night rings out with our laughter.

In this quaint little cabin, the rain bonds us closer together. Around the wooden table, we reminisce for the last time about our experiences and exchange jokes and stories. Youth has the taste of lemonade and the intensity of black coffee. How I regret having forsaken it for adulthood!

Today is the day! Luc brings me a pail of water so that Bach and I can take our last shower together. People are being very generous. Mr. Dông and young San, with whom I had an argument the other day, brought us two submarines from the market. Tuê and his brother also gave us two apples and two oranges. I am really very touched by all this kindness.

As we head for the harbour, Mr. Minh offers to carry our suitcase and almost everyone from the barrack accompanies us. The road is still muddy and slippery. Down the slope facing the sea, people are standing and waiting with their feet soaking in the wet grass. Beneath the canopied hangar where we first arrived in January, there is a row of empty desks and a roped-off passageway. None of the officials are here yet. The concrete dock which has now been completed, juts out to sea like an imposing peninsula.

I feel just as nervous as I did on my First Communion day. Everybody wants to have a few private moments with my brother and me. Mr. Minh keeps begging me to shed a tear. Bach's cousin, Thanh, calls me over in a grave voice. When I walk up to him, the look in his eyes makes me lower mine to the grass blades. "I have a friend who will be travelling to Canada with you. He speaks English. So when you get to Singapore he can phone Mr. Ben for you... I saw you crying several times behind the barrack...You remind me so much of my sister... Good-bye!"

When I look up, he has already disappeared down the road which is now part of my past. I feel something deep inside of me, yet I am not in love. Tuê drags me down to the dock to have my picture taken with his brother and my brother. With an expression of sincerity, he squeezes our shoulders and says that he is sorry he doesn't have any money to buy us new clothes. We make a pact – never to forget that we made the voyage together and to write always.

People are chatting in small groups. Most of them have accompanied us here to find out what their own departure will be like. Ky, one of the boys in our group, will also be leaving for Canada in two days, so we might see each other again. Standing next to our two friends, we watch the boats coming into the harbour.

The Indonesians are back at their desks and we are being asked to proceed with the formalities. Mr. Minh hands us our suitcase with fatherly tenderness. Mr. Cap discreetly slips me a note but I don't even bother looking at him. I only have eyes for Bach and Luc. I feel as though someone were cutting my umbilical cord again, reopening this primal wound which had been numbed by my subconscious. Is it worth leaving them behind for what I hope to find across the sea? Finally, I repeat the last words spoken to my mother, "I'm leaving."

When the customs officers search our suitcase from top to bottom, I am reminded of the times my mother secretly left the city to buy a few kilos of rice and the police would search her at the gate.

As we board the vessels, I feel as if we are climbing aboard a space ship which won't be returning to earth for a million years. While everybody is crying, the insensitive engines applaud. People on the dock (the island's protruding nose) are waving to us. My eyes are focused on our friends and I am licking the tears from my lips. They are warm and salty like the sea, like sweat...and blood... The panoramic view slowly recedes and fades out as it does in the final scene of a movie. Even though the sun is shining brightly, the sky is shedding a few tears, dispersing the crowd on the shore. The ship moves forward and I retreat. We see nothing but a long chain of islands resting like sleeping maidens, and thousands of foam-edged wavelets rippling forward in a collective dance formation. Once again, we have to get used to being on our own. When I hand my brother one of the submarine sandwiches, I notice that his eyes are moist too.

After we have eaten our submarines, the nausea, which I had forgotten about for three months, returns to take its toll. I am so anxious to arrive. Amid sky and sea, there is nothing but uninhabited islands. Oh, you miserable fool. Why must you spend your life in constant expectation. Every ounce of my energy is concentrating on controlling this gut-wrenching feeling. I wonder if life in America is worth all this suffering. In an effort to comfort me, a lady nearby hands me a small bottle of cinnamon oil to sniff but it only warms my nose and does nothing to relieve the nausea.

CHAPTER 18

SINGAPORE

Just before dawn, we land in Singapore. Our guides escort us from one room to another. My brother drags the suitcase and I, my feet. Then we board a crowded bus and I can see neither land nor sky. Again, I throw up in a plastic bag which I found along the way. In an almost agonizing voice I whisper to Thanh, "Would you please throw this away once we arrive?"

I must really look pitiful to him because he promptly answers, "Yes," with concern and sympathy.

The bus stops at the Singapore refugee camp. Pointing to the expanse in front of the Information Center, our guide informs us that we must stay here for four days before boarding a plane. Exhausted from the retching, I simply collapse in the first chair I spot while my brother goes to get our food for the evening and some money for the coming days.

We have to wait for the others to finish eating (once again) before we can borrow their dishes and beg for a bit of hot water to make ourselves a cup of instant noodle soup. Since the Information Center and verandah are already crowded, we have to sleep out in the yard on a makeshift bed (two chairs, face-to-face). I wonder if God is watching... I would like to tell Him to listen to the prayers of those I love – my family, Bach and Luc.

Feeling alone and abandoned, I shed solitary tears in the night. Crickets are calling the dew and the wind is chilling the air. I am hungry and my back hurts as I lie on these hard chairs. I can hear my brother turning over on his. He is all I have left now.

Before the sun's rays soak up the dew, we wake up. Tiny butterflies and dragonflies are dancing around the wild flowers, seemingly delighted with the new day. But our thoughts are plunged into the past and soaring above the skies of Galang and Saigon as we try to write to our loved ones. Our sentences and tears flow down onto the blue paper. We often have to stretch our aching muscles and cramped backs. Thanh's friend, as promised, tried to reach Mr. Ben by phone but without any luck. For breakfast, lunch and supper, we eat the bread and sweet milk which Bach bought for us.

There is one marvellous thing about Singapore: here, water runs freely from the taps! So we can shower two or three times a day. But it is pitch black inside the washroom and I am afraid. Bach isn't with me anymore. The evening slowly creeps in. We sleep the same way as last night but it is much cooler out tonight. In the middle of the night, raindrops come hammering down on our dreams, so we take shelter on the verandah. My brother manages to find room for his chair, whereas two girls about my age who were sleeping on the wooden platform move over to accommodate me.

A peddlar wakes us up with his tinkling bell, imitating the song of a brook. We buy a fresh bun from him and that will be our food for the day. In the afternoon, we go to the chapel to listen to a foreign priest who speaks Vietnamese. On the way, I have an opportunity to glimpse inside one of the brick houses into which four to eight families are crammed. Despite everything, I still think this is a luxurious camp.

The following day is rather mournful, and a lethargical mood pervades the camp. I become acquainted with the

154

gentleman who was sleeping next to me last night. After a long conversation about one thing and another, I finally find the courage to ask him what we should do about our false age problem. "Nothing. In America, the children are much bigger and taller, so don't worry," he says to reassure me.

All we eat today is our leftover bread and some fruit. I am saving an apple for Ky who is supposed to arrive from Galang tonight.

Next morning, on what will hopefully be our final day, I make it a point to go to the market with the other girls because we have had enough of eating only bread. For the first time in my life, I can understand just how insecure a deaf-mute person feels in a public place. We were barely able to make ourselves understood by the merchants when we tried to buy a bottle of soda and some cold cuts.

CHAPTER 19

FINAL DESTINATION

Around five o'clock in the afternoon, we all assembled to be driven to the airport. The bus we board wanders through busy streets full of high-rise buildings. The sun is setting gigantic clouds on fire. It is almost as though the Sodom catastrophy is being re-enacted. But down on the sidewalks, students in their uniforms are strolling by peacefully. They will soon be home and, unlike us, they know what to expect when they arrive home.

The airport looks foreign and ominous to me; the waiting rooms, people standing in line, machines, noises, lights, white lines and... I still don't know how I ended up sitting on the plane in this luxurious seat. Next to me is Ky and then my brother.

Rumor has it that we will be stopping in Tokyo, then on to Edmonton and finally...Montreal. My brother tells me that there are five hundred passengers on this Boeing 747. A message comes over the intercom in French, English, and then Spanish. Thunderstruck, I listen fearfully, but I still don't understand. Am I supposed to buckle this seat belt or not? Anyway, I don't know how. Oof! we are off. I am glued to the backrest and my ears are starting to hurt. All the familiar symptoms of sea-sickness raise their devilish heads.

I wake up often, feeling lost in this modern grotto where nightlights replace the stars. It is hard to believe that we are up in the clouds where birds come to rest their wings. Thanh's sleeping with his head drooping sideways and saliva is dribbling from the corner of his mouth – like when he was a child. The night seems longer than usual.

Light comes streaming through the portholes when the flight attendants serve us a hearty breakfast. The sight of food makes my stomach heave again and this horrible feeling gnaws at me throughout the flight! My menstrual period just started and I don't know where the washrooms are. I watch where the people go when they get up. After a time and much concentrated effort, I finally know where they are but I don't know how to operate them...

My head feels like a ton and my heart is in my throat. I am not the least bit impressed by the sight of Tokyo-the-splendid or Edmonton-the-unknown as glimpsed through the narrow porthole – it is too far from my aisle seat. I would have liked to check if there were any birds nests on the clouds as the songs say.

How many hours ago did we leave? My patience has almost reached the breaking point! A long time ago, I read a book about a young man who said to his sweetheart, "I'm learning to throw a lasso because I promised you the moon." Right now, I am learning to resign myself to loneliness because I promised my family "freedom"...

We are landing at last! Immediately, we board a bus. The wind is chilling me to the bones. Since I can't find a plastic bag, I have to use my serviette. Disgusted looks from the other passengers and the gloomy, gray asphalt make me cringe down into my seat.

We are being taken to a large hall whose ceiling and walls are made of glass. Out of respect for the people greeting us in clean suits and ties, I quickly hide my disgraceful serviette in my suitcase. Then we leave the "chic" place to board yet another bus. The heating and gas fumes make me soil my Norwegian sweater this time, while others empty their stomachs onto the floor. Wrapped in a warm coat, our Vietnamese guide doesn't seem perturbed by this. I don't know what to do about my vomit-filled suitcase now. My brother is deeply annoyed at me for doing this.

The scenery is quite a letdown. This country looks dead. The sun is hiding, empty desolate fields skirt the highway, trees are gray and bare like skeletons and there is not a single pedestrian on the sidewalks... I wonder if the air outside is breathable? I must stop looking at the panorama flashing by the window because it is making me dizzy and torturing my innards.

Our guide informs us that we will soon be arriving at the military camp in Longue-Pointe. With all this traipsing from one camp to another, I am starting to feel like a gypsy. But what they call a camp here looks more like a fortress comprised of massive buildings. The bus stops in front of one of these concrete boxes and we all rush inside to get out of the cold. The interior looks more like a hotel than a barrack like at Galang. Here, we are greeted by some tall Canadians in regal uniform, and several Vietnamese, whose skin is fairer than ours, dressed in their Sunday best.

We are asked to undress and to don paper robes and sandals. I find it both embarrassing and amusing. All the youngsters without parents are escorted together and led to separate rooms. The Canadian doctor comes to each room with an interpreter and gives us a general check-up. Around our wrists, he snaps on a plastic-covered paper bracelet bearing the date, our names and our ages. I feel terrible having to wear this constant reminder of my lie!

Next it is showering time. They pour some kind of product on our heads to eliminate every trace of lice. I don't mind because now I have nobody to play in my hair. So why keep them? Each one of us receives a lovely pair of pyjamas and a tooth brush.

Outside, the streetlights go on, projecting a lazy glow over the deserted street. Evening comes crawling in like a beggar in search of a refuge for the night. On my paper bracelet, they have printed 80/04/23; that means we left home exactly three months ago. "Now, this is no time to start brooding!" I mumble to myself.

After a good night's sleep, we are invited to have lunch in the cafeteria which is located in another building. It is freezing cold outside. One of the boys says he saw a thermometer which indicated four degrees celsius. A cafeteria is something totally new to me. The room is almost full; the men are wearing red pyjamas, the women's are blue, the soldiers' uniforms are green and the cooks' aprons' white. Trailing behind by brother, I feel like a tracked hare.

Here, they don't cut up the meat in small pieces like my mother used to do. The knife and fork are as difficult to manipulate as crutches. It would be so much simpler to eat with my fingers but the soldier at the next table is watching me. After the meal, we have to leave promptly in order to make room for the next group. Now I think I know what a cafeteria is. It is a restaurant where you can eat all you want without having to pay!

I spend the rest of the evening strolling down the streets with the other children. It is freezing cold in this country but I have to get used to it – this is my country now!

Sleep doesn't come easily tonight for I still feel like a stranger here. I am lying in a nice white bed which is like a nest made of soft and cosy blankets. Even the richest girl in my class back home never had this luxury. Yet I don't feel any happier than when I slept on two wooden chairs. My mind is fraught with anguish. What shall I do about our ages? And what is going to happen to us tomorrow?

We skip breakfast today in order to remain in bed awhile longer. This morning a Vietnamese of Chinese origin, Mr. La, comes to speak to us about life in Québec. He informs us about the public transportation system: buses, trains and subways. Here, unlike in Vietnam, fish and seafoods are considered luxury items; eggs are cheap but we mustn't eat too many because it is not good for our health. As far as other purchases go, it is always wiser to wait for sales.

Mr. La seems to have completed his exposé and now he is talking Chinese since most of the people are of Chinese origin. I wish he had talked about learning the language here, about employment and ...perhaps about our ages... Lord, grant me the courage to settle this problem once and for all! From among the Vietnamese ladies on the welcoming committee, I pick out the most affable one and follow her around for several hours before I can get enough nerve to say:

"Madam... During this trip, I lied about my age, what must I do? I feel like such a coward for not having told the truth. I declared that I was four years younger than I really am."

"We understand that. Tomorrow, all you have to do is have them make the necessary corrections when they process your papers."

And the lady walks off, looking impassive, while I remain standing there, dumbfounded. After all these months of anguish, the solution of my problem is so simple. I must go and tell my brother. We will both feel much better if we tell the truth! But not knowing what tomorrow may bring, still makes me cautious. After all, we are in a military camp...and that reminds me of conscription...

"Thanh, it doesn't make sense for us to reduce our ages by four years. Tomorrow, when they process our papers, I will declare myself one year younger and two less for you. And if the government won't help us after we're eighteen, then we'll study at night and work during the day to help out Mother."

My brother makes face and says, "You always make life so complicated. We could've left things as they were... But, if that's the way you want it, it's alright with me!"

So, now I am fourteen instead of fifteen and my brother is twelve instead of fourteen. If tomorrow they don't believe us, they will tell us. I am starting to feel better already.

In the afternoon, they distribute black plastic bags in which to put the clothing we are to receive. I am in paradise walking around this hall stocked with all sorts of new clothes. My lungs breathe in the scent of wool and cotton. A whole new life has begun for me. As I finger a pretty blouse on one of the shelves, a tear of joy wells up in the corner of my eye. From this day forward, nobody will ever scorn me because of my ragged clothes. While a charming Canadian lady with soft, smooth hands helps me try on some shoes, my mind races back to the time when my mother was busy repairing an old pair of shoes, found in the garbage, to wear to a wedding.

Back in our room, my brother and I admire our new wardrobes. When he tries on his woollen tuque, we both burst out laughing...

Time for the formalities. We have to sign so many papers. The officials agree to change our birth dates, as requested, no questions asked. Our problem is over! Bursting with excitement, I have to go outside because my joy is bigger than this building. I can't wait to live here, in a home with the people I love. It is cold, but my heart is still beating. Hope makes me realize that the leafless trees are not dead after all...

Since there is nothing to do between meals, we write a letter to our parents and gaze out the window facing the wall of an adjacent building. I wonder how we will ever manage to learn the language of this country? I try to listen to the voice coming from the TV set at the other end of the hall but it is drowned out by Vietnamese chit-chat. Apparently we spent thirty-seven hours on the plane before landing at Mirabel airport.

It is starting to look as though we have been abandoned in this camp. After supper in the cafeteria, a bus finally comes to take all the children who are alone, to the city. My first impressions of this country are soon dissolved by all these lights which defiantly brave the night and mock the sun and by the darling houses with their raised chimneys. Although the sidewalks are practically desolate and the trees are still gray and bare, I love this panorama where pines thrust their green pointed peaks towards the sky. Several cars roll by with serious faces at the wheel.

All seventeen of us enter a large building called Motel Merlin. Our guide, Mr. La, takes us up in the elevator. I don't like this shortcut because it makes me dizzy. We spend the night together in a large room where twenty red beds await us. I miss my nice blue pyjamas that disappeared in the wash. The lights are turned off and nobody explains what will happen to us next.

A refreshing shower starts the day off right. The girl next to me is complaining that the water is too hot, whereas I find it rather cold. I don't think I have ever washed up so quickly. Together with the three other Catholics in the group, Thanh and I walk over to a nearby church. Strangely enough, the people don't seem surprised to see us there. Is it out of respect or out of indifference? Oh, if only we could sing in this foreign language! I brought some money for the collection but since I don't know the value of these coins, I am confused about how much to give.

On our way back, we idly stroll down the streets, peering into the shops with our noses pressed against the windows and our eyes building dreams.

Back at the motel, Mr. La gathers everyone around him and informs us that we all will be living with Québec families. I throw a smiling glance at Thanh – we will have Canadian parents! Miss Hoa would like us to tell her about our hopes and dreams. Since ours has already come true, to be part of a family again, we say nothing. But I am moved to hear one of the boys talk of his dream of becoming a pianist – three of his fingers were amputated while he was working in a sawmill. Mr. La then interviews us privately. He writes down our whole story and our plans for the future. Our new parents are both teachers who are childless. How much luckier can we get!

A charming Canadian lady comes to pick us up in her van – Thanh, Ky, another boy called Liêm and myself. Because of the curtained windows, we feel totally disoriented. But it doesn't matter. We happily share our dreams for the future as we would a birthday cake. My brother and I will have parents who are professors, Liêm's new father is a doctor and Ky will be part of a family of five girls. Through the rear-view mirror, the lady is smiling at us.

In the living room of her house, she introduces us to our adoptive parents. They are both wearing glasses and broad, friendly smiles. Our first words in French to them are papa and maman! These two words, uttered in a tremulous and shaky voice, sound true and they will eventually erase all differences between us.

Suddenly, I realize that I am born again and remember that God was the first to want me!

On this Sunday, April 27th, 1980, a new life begins for us!

CHAPTER 20

CANADA

Time, the invisible giant who makes the seasons swing round in a farandole, brings us summer thunderstorms, winter blizzards, autumn leaves and spring thaw. Eight calendars have marked the days of my life away from my native Vietnam. My Canadian parents have spared nothing to make me feel the heartbeat of this new country. They have shared their language and their ideas and I no longer feel like a stranger. Now, when I say the words "papa" and "maman", I really feel I belong to this family and to this country that has welcomed me with open arms. I have learned to overcome many cultural barriers and to live without the mask of pride. There were problems and misunderstandings but I am now able to resolve them through dialogue.

It seems like yesterday that I came to live in my new parents' house in Rivière-des-Prairies, away from the big city highways and high rises. Armed with a dictionary on that first night, Thérèse and Normand showed us their home. Numbed by feelings of fear and insecurity, I tried to understand the flood of words. I searched for and found the courage to like these strangers. That evening, I helped my adoptive mother to cook the supper meal. She was boiling the rice the same way that we did in Vietnam except that it was in a shiny pot and on a sophisticated stove. She showed me how to coat the chicken legs with spiced bread crumbs and to place them in the oven. I carefully copied all her gestures as we set the table. She instructed me on the use of each utensil, making me repeat the names of every object that we were touched. I was trying my best to register them in my mind – rice, pot, stove, fork. At the table, Thanh and I were stunned as we were each given a chicken leg. In a jumble of French, English and sign language, we explained that in Vietnam a chicken leg was a meal for the entire family and only for special occasions.

I had so much to say about my past and so much to ask about the future but the words to express myself were beyond my grasp. A simple smile seemed inadequate. The meal was excellent but, not wanting to appear impolite, I did not eat very much.

After dinner our "papa" took out some paper and pens and showed us how to write our names and how to pronounce them. Thérèse seemed to have a natural gift for Vietnamese sounds (I later found out that she had several Vietnamese students in her class). I also wrote down a few words to be telegraphed to my family in Vietnam. After that, we were quiet; it was getting tiresome to converse. We went into the living room to watch television. Seeing that we didn't understand the show, our parents began our first formal French lesson. "Maman marche, papa joue de la guitare, debout, assis, cheveux, nez, bouche, oreilles..." And we repeated and repeated, trying to comprehend the gestures accompanying the sounds.

At bedtime, they showed us how the light switch, shower and toilet worked and then walked us to our respective bedrooms. All alone in this big bed I missed my little sisters terribly. The thought of ghosts made me hide under the thick blankets. In my prayers, I wondered if Jesus could understand every language on the earth? If only He could be like the genie of Aladdin's lamp and bring all my family into this comfortable house.

During the next few days, I slept for long hours at a time. After the initial fatigue from the long journey wore off, I was overwhelmed with the constant barrage of discoveries. My new country was a wonderful land of stores. There was enough merchandise to dress the entire city of Saigon. The things we had seen in the catalogues given to us by the American soldiers were not just dreams. Here, in Canada, heaven is no illusion. I had ten dollars left from the Immigration money. I couldn't decide if I should buy a shirt for my father or pants for my little brother. In the end, I chose luxury over practicality – underwear for my mother and sisters.

Trang, a student from Thérèse's class, accompanied me on that first shopping trip. She was pretty, spoke French well and had arrived here with all her family in 1975. It was hard for me not to feel somewhat envious. Acting as an interpreter for Thérèse, Trang asked me to try on some skirts and blouses. I thought the clothes were far too showy but I didn't dare refuse and risk hurting Thérèse's feelings. Trang told me that my foster mother was spending a week's salary on my new clothes. We went to find my brother who was shopping with Normand. He had difficulty finding a pair of shoes that fit. Even after trying on five or six pairs, the chosen pair still made him walk like Charlie Chaplin. Poor Thanh! He never wore anything but sandals and then, only for school and church.

During our first week in Canada, many friends, relatives and neighbours came to visit us. I got to know and love these people who shared their time with me. However, their Western custom of kissing one another as a form of greeting made me feel rather uncomfortable at first. Visitors often brought clothing that didn't fit their children anymore. I felt much better wearing these clothes because I had the impression I was saving lots of money.

After a few weeks, I began to feel the pressure of having parents again. I wondered why my new parents were always right. If their wishes were orders, why couldn't mine be orders too? I had played the role of an adult for many years and now I was a child again. My parents didn't like to see me crying but I was inconsolable. I wasn't used to their direct way of expressing themselves. Unconsciously, I began to do whatever I could to be unpleasant to my parents. Maybe it was to test how much they cared about me? One day, they said that if Thanh and I were not happy, they would have to find a new home for us where they could be sure of our happiness. But it wouldn't be any easier somewhere else. I had to accept their rules in order to learn how to live here. They were strict parents but we knew it was for our own good.

One month after we arrived, we received our first letter from Vietnam. Our adoptive parents were as anxious to listen to the translation of the letter as we were to read the news. Even our next door neighbour and her children came over to hear the news about my family. On an old brown piece of paper, my mother relayed the joy my Vietnamese family felt when they learned that Thanh and I were alive. To celebrate the event, she killed our dog Keo so they would have some meat for dinner. To repay the debt of our passage, she had to sell her sewing machine, my violin and all the beds in the house. As I was translating this, everybody started to cry. Since my mother had volunteered to tell the authorities about our escape, the government merely cut their ration of rice, as punishment. It could have been much worse. A few other members of my family had apparently also chosen the same path of freedom but they ended up at the bottom of the ocean, or in jail.

Shortly after that letter arrived, we spent our first weekend in the country. I was elated by all the wide open space that was ours to enjoy. I spent the weekend transplanting seedlings and feeling as if I possessed a certain power over nature. I wanted to write everything about this weekend to my family but couldn't bring myself to. It would have been unfair to tell them of my good fortune when I knew that they barely had enough to eat in Vietnam. I only wrote that I loved them and that I would work hard to be accepted here.

The summer was not to be a holiday. We had to learn French as soon as possible and our adoptive parents spent their entire vacation teaching us the language. Thérèse was the grammar specialist, while Normand searched for concrete ways of helping us understand the difficult words. As my language skills improved, the communication gap closed. I was able to tell them about my past experience and about what I had learned since I arrived. They also helped me discover their wonderful culture, making me breathe the country's poetry with artists like Félix Leclerc and Gilles Vigneault. I was proud to understand French.

I was amazed to see how much freedom is allowed in Canada. There are no curfews, permission is not required to go from one town to another, and the police don't check up on overnight guests in one's home. Political freedom was also new to me. In Vietnam, I had felt and seen the terrible affects that restraint of this basic human right had on the people. The Quebec independence referendum was my first opportunity to witness such freedom. It was a refreshing change for me as I watched the media, the political parties and the general population, voice opposing views and exercise their individual rights.

Certain western customs astonished me. At one of our first Christmas family gatherings, the guests danced and played cards. Our host served wine with the meal. After the evening, my brother asked our foster parents if those people were real Catholics because, in Vietnam, priests condemned such practices. They replied that in this country, such activities are not considered sinful: the wine underlines the happy occasions, dancing expresses the joy of those assembled and the card game just adds to the fun.

New Year's night was also an evening of discovery. I watched the guests moving their bodies to the rhythm of the music. With a little persuasion, I too joined in and found myself having a wonderful time. My first Christmas and New Year's was a happy one for me. I was glad to be a part of this big family, but I could not helping thinking about my real family.

This obsession with my sister family in Vietnam remains with me even today. The best of moments still have a sour taste. The hope that my family in Vietnam will someday be united with my family in Canada gives me strength. I am responsible for not only my own life but also the lives of seven people in South East Asia. They sacrificed their food to help me escape. For the past few years, I have been eating well, have been loved, and have clothes that keep me warm and dry. I am in university and have a promising future. Back in Vietnam, they are struggling to find enough food to survive.

I arrived here as a beggar in search of a new life, guided more by my instinct for survival than the wisdom of my fifteen summers. Canada offered me the freedom I set out to find. I am indebted to my adoptive parents, their respective families, my teachers and new friends, for my apprenticeship as a Canadian. I am proud to be citizen of this great land. I have a new country to serve, a new family to love, and a new life to build.

EPILOGUE

On Sunday, April 27, 1980, we welcomed two Vietnamese teenagers into our home. They spoke neither French nor English. The only French words they could utter were "papa" and "maman". In no time, we came to know and love them as our own for they were both so loving, and determined to learn and work.

Doan and Thanh told us their story and helped us get to know the people they love. Their dream speaks of these people who fill their hearts and we came to espouse that dream. Because of this deep attachment to their recent past, we asked Doan – whose literary skills were evident – to write about her voyage "from Vietnam to Canada." It is important for the reader to note that she set out to write this account of their adventures, in French, after merely two years of studies in that language. During her last two summer vacations, she was able to complete this book. Incredible...but true! Having witnessed its gradual gestation with awe and joy, we can honestly say that she did it all on her own.

As she produced this narrative, we had the opportunity of learning more about their past experiences and about their family. Together, we now long for the day when the whole family will be reunited once again.

Today, we now have a better understanding of the refugee situation throughout the world. We sincerely hope that Doan's testimony in *Escape From Vietnam* will open more doors and hearts in response to the cries for "help". As for us, our children have helped stretch our hearts to a global dimension and our desire to fraternize with the whole universe has taken on a new intensity because of Doan and Thanh.

Thérèse and Normand
Adoptive parents

Printed by
the workers of
Ateliers Graphiques Marc Veilleux Inc.
Cap-Saint-Ignace, Qué.